KIND TRANSPARENCY

Kind Transparency

Amanda Frye

Copyright © 2024 by Amanda Frye
All rights reserved. No part of this book may be reproduced in any manner whatsoever without written permission except in the case of brief quotations embodied in critical articles and reviews.
First Printing, 2024

Epigraph

> *"Any sufficiently advanced technology is indistinguishable from magic."*
> Arthur C. Clark

Have you ever witnessed someone handle a situation so seamlessly that you were left in awe? Was it a level of sorcery, a puzzle waiting to be solved, or simply a mystery craving an answer? Here's the secret: it's not magic at all. Once you uncover the mechanics of engagement, that veil of mystique fades away. You start thinking, "hey, I could totally do that..."

But there's a catch – you have to **want** to peek behind the curtain.

Now, recall your most cherished relationships. What sets them apart? Was it the glitz and glamour? The constant whirlwind of excitement? Maybe in some moments, but probably not. Chances are, it's the person who understood you at your core, who embraced your quirks and flaws without hesitation.

We all yearn for genuine connections and understanding. Sadly, our world tends to glorify screens and social facades, perpetuating a distorted version of real human interaction.

In these pages, we embark on a journey of self-discovery and unapologetic revelations. Through stories, facts, a dash of fun, and even a few logic bombs, we will unravel the elusive "people magic." It's a journey toward understanding and connection, a path that leads us to the heart of authentic interactions.

We're going from magic to mastery!

Acknowledgements

My mother existed in her own lane. She was steadfast in her beliefs, never minced words, and you always knew where you stood with her.

Now, she was from another time, a time where people had biases and didn't consider other people's feelings or alternative viewpoints. A time when women were not regarded as equal, nor did they have a voice in most decisions. And at that time, she grew up in poverty, with little education; and could barely read until my father taught her in their late teens. Despite all this, she always stood up for what she believed (sometimes to a fault) and spoke her mind. But because of it, she was remarkably open-minded to the ideas of the day, and never stopped learning.

She told me many hard truths over the years, ones that I didn't want to hear but needed to. She did it in her way, which could be abrasive, harsh, and out of nowhere. So, there were definitely people out there that didn't appreciate it. In those scenarios, she was more than happy to cut those people out of her life. This is where we differ.

What I've observed, taking the best pieces of who she was, along with the trial and error of my life, is that you can have it both ways. You can say what you mean, without being a jerk.

To the unapologetic spirit of my mother,

In a world where people often tiptoed around truths, you were a beacon of authenticity. Your beliefs were unwavering, your words unfiltered, and your stance crystal clear. You thrived in a different era, one marred by biases and where empathy sometimes took a backseat. It was a time when women's voices were silenced, and opportunity was a rare visitor. A time when poverty held hands with limited education, and literacy was a gift that arrived late. Yet, against these odds, you stood tall, fighting for your convictions, and never allowing the currents of circumstance to sway you.

You dished out truths, some as tough as nails, but they were the medicine needed for growth. Your delivery? Blunt, unvarnished, and often without warning. Sure, not everyone embraced it – your approach ruffled feathers and stirred the pot. And when it did, you wielded the knife of detachment without hesitation, trimming away negativity from your life. It's an art of self-preservation that I've witnessed, admired, yet tweaked to match my own stride.

As I journey through life, I've woven threads of your legacy with my own experiences – a tapestry of boldness, vulnerability, and, yes, maintained a touch of sass. I've learned that honesty doesn't have to don a mask of harshness, that candor can exist alongside kindness. And that's the gem I've polished from your diamond mine of wisdom – the ability to speak my mind without severing ties.

So, here's to you, a woman ahead of your time, an embodiment of candid courage. In these pages, I weave your spirit with mine, stitching a road map that honors both your unapologetic grit and the gentle power of communication that Kind Transparency stands for. It's a fusion of the past and the present, a testament to the truth that, indeed, you can say what you mean without being a jerk. Here's to rewriting the rules of communication with a dash of kindness.

With love and a touch of your magic,
Amanda

In memory of Ruth Crosby.
May 2nd, 1944 – May 15th, 2019

Dedication

To my husband,

As I wade through the delightful chaos of this life, I can't help but think of you and the incredible role you play. You, my dear, are the unsung hero in this narrative.

Late nights conversations with disheveled ideas, and mad scientist monologues. That's me. But you? You're the patient soul who not only tolerates the madness but embraces it with open arms. You're the reason my late-night musings don't end up in the trash.

You've witnessed my highs and lows, from the euphoria of a breakthrough to the frustration of defeat. And through it all, you've been a rock-solid pillar of support, occasionally offering chocolate, sympathy, and random excursions.

In this grand adventure of our life, you're not just a character; you're the comic relief, the moral compass, and the heartwarming ending all rolled into one. Your unwavering faith in me is like the plot twist I never saw coming, making every chapter of our story richer and more vibrant.

So, here's to you, my muse, my partner in crime, and the love of my life. With you by my side, the story is just beginning, and I can't wait to see where it takes us next. With love, laughter, and infinite gratitude...

In every universe,

Amanda

Contents

Epigraph — v
Acknowledgements — vii
Dedication — ix

Preface — 1
1. Kind Transparency — 7
2. Words that actually matter — 17
3. The Human Blueprint — 39
4. Digging Deeper — 55
5. Why does it happen? — 67
6. People don't change — 77
7. Sometimes people are a$$holes — 93
8. Embrace the chaos — 109
9. Words matter, still — 117
10. Care anyway — 125
11. It's not a fad — 133

Closing — 138
Additional Resources — 141
About the Author — 142
Notes — 143

Preface

Hey, look at you, diving headfirst into the pages of Kind Transparency!

I wanted to open this book with a beautifully written soliloquy of words that would wrap you up with excitement, suspense, and wonder. But instead, I sat, and stared at a blank screen, writing, and rewriting until the pure idea of my sanity was in question. Because let's be real here. Writing a book? What was I thinking? It's like trying to find the light switch in a pitch-black room. You grope around haphazardly, stub your toe on uncertainty, and wonder if you'll ever get out of the dark.

Seriously, why didn't they teach us this in school? You'd think there would be a guidebook somewhere, right? Oh - wait... they did, and there is. There are literally thousands of resources dedicated to this exact thing. But that doesn't make it any easier, does it? Then it hit me. This is the opening, this is the whole concept, this is what we need to discuss.

I'm human. You are human. We are all human, and the world is hard. It doesn't come with a set of instructions or a universal road-map. Sure, there are rules, guidebooks, and training manuals along the way that offer some sense of guidance. But that doesn't mean every person is going to grasp everything immediately (or ever) and that's OK. We are not born with any of the answers, so it's perfectly normal to stumble, make mistakes, and learn as we go. That is what this book is about. It's about understanding how different people interpret their own training manuals, and that those guidebooks are written one page at a time throughout our lives.

Being human means that we are a work in progress. We're constantly evolving, figuring things out, and finding our way through this ever more complex world. So, don't be too hard on yourself or anyone else for that matter. We're all in this together, trying to make sense of it all. THAT is what we are going to explore here. People are never perfect, and neither is communication. So, before we begin, we need to wipe our slates clean of any assumptions or expectations we have going in of people, process, and change.

No, really. Take a moment to envision the imaginary chalk board in your mind. The one you use to tally up your list of people who have slighted you. Your subliminal notes to yourself. That personal burn book you've been amassing over the years.

Next, I want you to imagine yourself. If someone else were to describe you as a person, what would you want them to say? What would they really say? How big is the gap between those two things?

(I don't know about you, but I like to think of myself as the anti-Mary Poppins, "Practically (im)perfect in every way!")

Do you think other people's description of you would change if they saw your chalkboard? We all have things on it that we wouldn't want others to see. But so do they. Everyone is experiencing a life that we know very little about. So, let's give ourselves the advantage of going into this discussion with a clean board, making room for new notes.

Maybe this is the start of something beautiful. Or maybe it's just the beginning of a long and winding road filled with awkward metaphors and self-deprecating humor. Either way, I promise we'll figure it out together, and if nothing else, we've already explored the uncharted territory of me not knowing how to start a book.

Why are you reading this?

I really want to know what actually brought you to this intriguing crossroads of self-discovery and candid communication? Fair warning, there will be no beating around the bush here; we're ripping off band-aids and opening old wounds. You're here for a reason – whether it's looking for answers, solutions, or maybe it's just a sprinkle of that 'people magic' that's piqued your interest. But, before we can openly connect with others, we must connect with ourselves. So, your first mission, if you choose to accept it, is to figure out your WHY.

Now, this isn't just any ordinary everyday why. This is that deep, nagging, squeaking shopping-cart wheel of a why, and it's going to be your GPS guiding you through this process.

- Was it the siren call of poor communication that led you here?
- Are your words trapped in the cage of your mind, turning your conversations into puzzles with missing pieces?
- Perhaps you're tired of feeling like your voice is a whisper lost in the noise, and you long for someone who will genuinely listen.
- Maybe you're in a bind? You're navigating through life's labyrinth, and every path you take seems like a dead end?
- Are you tired of being a doormat, letting others trample over you?
- Saying "no" feels like an alien concept, and you're yearning to reclaim your boundaries?
- What about the precarious human dance with anger – is it a tango you're ready to give up?
- Are you craving a way to express yourself without lessening who you really are?
- Did someone – a friend, a mentor, or maybe even that wise barista at your local coffee shop – nudge you toward this book? (Because that would be awesome!)

Or could it be, dear reader, that you've heard whispers about me, and my knack for blending wisdom with a dash of fun? It's okay, you can admit it – you're secretly hoping this book lives up to the hype. (me too)

And hey, if by any chance you think I'm less of a sage and more of a hack, well, kudos for the bravery! You're reading this to prove a point, and who knows, you might uncover some golden nuggets of wisdom that surprise even your skeptical heart.

Regardless of your "why," here's the deal: you've taken the first step on a journey toward a kinder, more transparent you.

We will begin by unraveling the mysteries of communication, boundaries, and the magic of genuine connection. So, grab a coffee, your PJ's, or your favorite stuffed animal because we are about to get comfortable with stepping outside of our comfort zone.

Why did I write this?

Now, let's delve into the reasons that "Kind Transparency" found its way from thought to ink. Throughout the book, we're going to get personal – a glimpse into my mind, my motives, and the very core of why this book came to life.

Selfish, you might think, and you're not entirely wrong. This book is, in a way, a dialogue with myself, a way to unravel my own thoughts and emotions. Putting pen to paper was my way of untangling the intricate web of my own feelings, weaving them into words, sentences, and stories that resonated with my truth. Then hoping they could help others get there faster than I did.

And then there's the quest to re-center. Life is like a whirlwind, constantly tugging us in different directions. Writing "Kind Transparency" was my way of anchoring myself amidst the chaos. It forced me to pause, reflect, and realign my own goals with the values that have become the heartbeat of Kind Transparency.

But, I didn't just write this book for me. It's a beacon for anyone who's navigated the complexity of emotions, the turbulence of relationships, and the rollercoaster of life. If these words can be a lantern guiding someone else through their moments of uncertainty, then my mission will be accomplished.

Drawing from my career and life experience has proven to be a treasure trove of insights. From boardrooms to brainstorming sessions, I've witnessed countless instances where a simple conversation, or a transparent exchange of thoughts could have completely redirected the course of events. This book is my attempt to sprinkle a bit of confetti – the art of open, honest communication – into the world.

So, here we are, you and I, united in this task. My why, your curiosity - our shared journey. Let's explore the complexity of human connections, untangle the knotted mess of Christmas lights that is communication, and maybe – just maybe – uncover a gem or two that resonates with the very essence of why we are here.

Let's jump in...

1

Kind Transparency

As a leader, of course it's my job to keep the clients satisfied, but more than that, it's my *duty* to make sure that my team and those around us are comfortable and safe. **Not happy.**

Let's start by declaring - It is not your job to make sure everyone is happy 100% of the time. It's just not going to happen. You are not going to be happy every moment of every day, and neither are the people around you. Once you square with that, you give yourself permission to let go. Let go of these outdated notions that we exist to please other people, or that confrontation must be avoided at all costs.

Your team and those closest to you are your most important customers. Your passion should be to give them an environment for success. However, success does NOT mean hand holding, walking on eggshells or pandering to everyone in an effort to keep the peace. It does mean that we will take an approach which prioritizes understanding people, their motivations, their communication style and tolerances. With this, we can set strong boundaries WHILE maintaining trust and respect. The hard part is that this means different things for different people.

It doesn't matter if you're a team lead, coach, mentor, manager, or executive. You have to put in the work, with intention. Sure, it gets easier and more organic over time, but you have to find your style and your voice.

Over the years, there are a few things that have become apparent to me as a participant and outside observer of social contracts: (Feel free to chant them.)

1. You can be amazing at what you do, but if you can't communicate effectively and motivate others to join you, it's all for nothing. (Yes I said *join* you, not *follow* you. This is a relay race, not a cult - ~~strike the chanting.~~)
2. <u>And this could not be more evident;</u> most people are reluctant to speak up. Consider this fact in combination with things like a new team, new project, or new tools and you have a recipe for what I like to call "The Coyote Syndrome". If you remember the Road Runner cartoon, Wile E. Coyote is **ever present, constantly engaged** and **actively working on his tasks**, but <u>never gets what he wants</u>. The same thing happens when people are too uncomfortable or afraid to voice their opinions.
3. Most people are incredibly passionate about what they do, and they care <u>so much</u> about the success of what they are doing. **Until they don't.** Usually because they no longer feel valued and heard.
4. Passion breeds disagreement. If no one cared, there would be nothing to disagree about. So, while it can be frustrating, constructive debate fuels innovation, and is the ultimate catalyst to a high functioning team.

"Never push loyal people to the point where they don't give a damn."
- Peter Drucker

We have to remember that people experience the world through their own paradigms, and people intrinsically act from their own motivations. We are all saying the same things and are marching toward the same goals. But sometimes it's hard to see that when you're so close to it, and it's easy to get caught up in pride and ego. There isn't always a right answer, there is just an answer for the moment, given everything we know, and it's ok to disagree. It's even ok to be wrong, as long as we move forward.

Starting with this framework we can define Kind Transparency in this way:

> **The ability to read and learn the motivations and triggers of those around you in order to identify how to best communicate complex ideas and gain buy-in.**

Ok, that sounds like every piece of communication advice you've ever heard right? Wrong. Because you have to take it two steps further to really affect change.

> **Then leveraging these targeted communication models to build trust, while setting distinct boundaries of acceptable engagement and behavior.**

And then...

> **Redirecting unacceptable behavior towards positive outcomes by reaffirming the person's motivations and basic needs.**

What does that mean exactly?

1. Connect with people on a genuine personal level (Actually care)
2. Understand the personality markers that drive them to feel and act the way that they do
3. Define the persons basic motivators and needs
4. Create a safe place for people to exist
5. Listen to their concern, and acknowledge
6. Outline the boundaries, where they have crossed them, and your feelings about their actions
7. Define acceptable tolerance for boundaries
8. Discuss options where their needs can be met within the boundary
9. Follow-up with positive reinforcement for behavior, or start over (with reduced boundaries)

Story Time

Before I dive in here, I want to prepare you for many stories like this throughout the book. I could discuss theory all day long, but it's exceptionally hard to put these ideas into practice without context and examples. The names and identifying details of certain individuals and events have been changed to protect the innocent. However, for those who were there with me - #IYKYK

(Theme song from Cops fades out in the distance)

This book wouldn't exist without the conversation that coined the phrase "Kind Transparency". That conversation came at the end of a precariously long week which was marred by conflict. At the time, I was leading a PMO and helping to Program manage some of our larger brands. One program in particular had a high level of visibility and was incredibly delicate from an account management perspective. Without giving away any trade secrets, there was a large software project, for a very large customer, and it was in total disarray. We were exhausted and fighting a slow, tedious uphill battle. Despite our best efforts, the client wasn't happy. We weren't happy. It had gone stagnate.

The only way to move forward included a drastic change in scope. We weren't getting any of the answers we needed, and deadlines were closing in on us. Unfortunately, we had made some assumptions that ended up not being true.

(You know what happens when we make assumptions - we just talked about this...)

In the simplest of terms, the customers' internal systems were older and more disparate than expected, which made it incompatible with what we were trying to build. There was a way forward. We had options. But, this required a series of things to happen, in a certain order, all of which we had no control over.

First, we needed to custom build a new login system for them. Secondly, we needed them to update several of their databases so we could access the information that we needed to integrate the two applications properly. We were completely roadblocked and dependent on the customer to take this action.

Realizing this, we needed to raise the red flag. We had a different, more looming problem though. There was significant political pressure surrounding this account. We constantly felt the *overarching message to "not rock the boat". This project, while big in its own right, was just a small part of a larger engagement. Our marching orders were to make it work, make them happy, - say **YES**. I unfortunately am unable to not say things when they are important, which was surely to the detriment to my manager at the time.

<Insert super heartfelt apology for being a difficult employee here>

Could we have made it work? Probably, but it would have caused issues in the future, caused security concerns, and ultimately was not scalable. So, we set up a call with the customer to address the problems.

This was a big call. 8-10 people invited from each side...

You know those days when it feels like sh*t is going to hit the fan, and it's a handheld fan, and you're the one standing there holding it? Yeah, it was one of those days. We had a project spiraling out of control, our customers' frustration was practically oozing through the phone lines, and the executives on our side were nervously staring a deep hole right into the pit of our souls.

My team looked at me like I had the magic answer hidden somewhere in my back pocket (spoiler alert: I didn't). But I knew that the only way out of this mess was through it, and that meant one thing: having a brutally honest, transparent conversation. So, I geared up, took a deep breath, and jumped off the deep end.

This wasn't one of those "let's sugarcoat the truth and hope they don't notice" moments. Nope, I laid it all out—concerns, risks, the likelihood of things blowing up if we didn't make some changes. I'm talking about the kind of honesty that makes your palms sweat. I expected them to be defensive, and to get strong push-back, because people don't like to admit when they are wrong. The other option I was prepared for was them nodding politely and blowing me off. To my surprise, neither of those things happened; they actually listened. They took accountability for the age of their systems, the inconsistency of data, and their part in the delays.

Crazy, right?

We walked through all the options, discussed what each path would mean (and yeah, I might've thrown in a few dramatic pauses for effect), and we adjusted the timelines to something more realistic. I was fully expecting the usual "Why are you wasting my time?" response, but instead, the customer thanked us. I'm not kidding. They were genuinely appreciative. And then, they did something no one saw coming—they expanded our scope to address some of the issues I pointed out, because they didn't have the time or bandwidth to resolve them on their own. Which meant more work (and more money) for us.

After we hung up, I walked back into my office like a heavy weight champion, proudly showing off my new belt. We then had a quick debrief, where my CIO at the time, clearly stunned, asked, "What just happened?!?!" And without missing a beat, I smirked and said, "That was Kind Transparency."

And just like that, it became a thing. People started using it, and it spread faster than office gossip. The term stuck, and it's now a part of everything that I do. So, I decided to take all this magic, wrap it up, and put it in this book. That way, you too can experience the thrill of navigating life with a little bit of honesty, a lot of kindness, and the occasional sweaty palms.

So, here we are. You've made it through the first chapter, probably thinking, "Alright, I get it. People are messy, communication's important, blah blah blah." But seriously, stick with me here. We've barely scratched the surface, and if you think the people around you are complicated, wait until we start talking about **you**.

Yes, you. The one holding this book and thinking you've got it all figured out. (Spoiler alert: you don't. Hell, I don't) But that's okay—none of us do. And that's the point! If you were expecting a neat, little bow-tie solution to all your communication problems, that doesn't exist. This is a process. And you're gonna mess it up. We all do. But you're also gonna get better each time you do it, if you're willing to put in the work. (If you're not? Well, good luck with your surface-level small talk and avoidance issues.)

But before we go any further, I want to leave you with this: **you've got this**. I don't care if you've been dodging difficult conversations like they're the plague or if you think you're too set in your ways to change. If you're reading this, you're already doing the work. You're making the choice to show up. And that? That's the hardest part.

Alright, enough of the warm and fuzzies. In the next two chapters we'll get into the real meat of how to take everything you're learning here and actually **apply it**. Don't worry, I'll walk you through it step by step, because, frankly, if I don't, you'll just keep doing the same crap you've been doing, and we both know how that's been working out.

2

Words that actually matter

There are four key words that I want you to remember throughout Kind Transparency. You might be thinking, "Great, more corporate buzzwords to add to my growing list," but hold on—these aren't just words. They're the key to every meaningful interaction you'll ever have, whether it's at work, at home, or with that random cashier at the coffee shop who constantly overshares.

Words Matter.

Communication isn't as simple as having a mouth and using it. If it were, everyone would be an expert by now, right? It takes skill and experience to know when to speak up, when to shut up, and how to choose your words so they land where they're supposed to. (Spoiler alert: that's SO MUCH harder than it sounds.) But don't worry, soon you're going to be able to tackle this all on your own!

By the end of this chapter, you'll learn the framework of how to better wield your words like a well-sharpened sword, avoid the pitfalls of poorly thought-out communications, and become the kind of person who not only gets the point across but does so in a way that doesn't leave a trail of destruction in your wake. So, let's talk about what makes communication truly effective, and explore how you can become the master of 'saying what you mean—without being a jerk.'

The 4 C's of Kind Transparency

Communication	Collateral
Coordination	Consistency

Communication:

Imagine a world without words. A place where every thought, feeling, and intention is trapped inside, with no way out. Sounds like a nightmare, right? A world of isolation, where misunderstandings thrive and opportunities die before they even get a chance to breathe. But, the good news is: **we don't live in that world.** So, why does it still sound so familiar?

We have the ability to communicate, but most people still struggle like they're tongue-tied. Fear, insecurity, doubt—they creep in and choke us before we can get the words out. You know the feeling. You want to say something, but you're scared. Scared of rejection, scared of confrontation, scared of looking weak, scared of being misunderstood. So what do you do? You stay silent, or worse—you tiptoe around the real issue, hoping someone else will just magically understand what's going on in your head. Spoiler alert: they won't.

Here's the opportunity: every single time you open your mouth, you have the chance to connect, build trust, or make sh*t happen. But it requires you to be fearless. It requires you to stop dodging, stop sugarcoating, and start speaking with purpose. If you want to get anywhere—personally, professionally, or otherwise—you have to learn to own your communication. You've got to drop the BS and say what you actually mean.

Communication isn't just important—it's non-negotiable. However, it is important to remember that every word we say carries weight—whether it's a gentle nudge, a full-blown confession, or even that offhand comment you thought no one noticed. Like I tell my husband when I make him Diabetic friendly desserts:

> "It's sugar free, not consequence free."
> (If you don't know the consequences, google sugar free gummy bear reviews... you won't be disappointed)

The same goes for communication in real life. Just because you have the freedom to speak your mind doesn't mean you're exempt from the repercussions. Words can build bridges or burn them; they can mend relationships or tear them apart. It's not about censoring yourself—it's about understanding the impact, taking responsibility, and choosing your words wisely. The ripple effect of your communication is far-reaching, and the consequences are as real as that sugar-free gummy bear experience you wish you could now forget.

When you speak, people listen (whether you think they do or not). And what you say lingers—it can either lift someone up or send them spiraling. The consequences of your words are as real as that sugar-free gummy bear situation you'll wish you could forget. So, choose wisely. Which brings us to **Collateral**—because every word you put out there has a price, and it's time to start thinking about the cost.

Collateral:

The collateral of communication represents the impact and aftermath of our words and actions. We understand that the effects of communication ripple beyond the immediate moment, shaping perceptions and relationships. We strive to choose our words thoughtfully, recognizing that what we say—or choose not to say—can leave a lasting impression. Just as skyscrapers are meticulously designed, our collateral is carefully considered, aiming to foster positive outcomes and build trust within our community.

Imagine a conversation as a stone dropped into a calm pond. The initial splash creates ripples that spread outward, touching everything in their path. These ripples are the collateral of conversation – the effects and consequences that extend far beyond the words exchanged. Just as a stone's impact on water shapes the pond's surface, our words shape the dynamics, perceptions, and relationships between individuals. The collateral of conversation is the unseen force that lingers, influencing emotions, opinions, and the intricate interplay of human connection. Here, we will explore how the echoes of our words leave a lasting imprint on the waters of our interaction.

Let's define collateral, shall we? Collateral has several meanings, all of which fit the concept I'm trying to convey about communication and interpersonal dynamics, making it the perfect C for our list.

Col·lat·er·al (A lesser known definition)

- Situated at the side: belonging to the side or to what is at the side; hence, occupying a secondary or subordinate position.
- Acting indirectly; acting through side channels.
- Accompanying; attendant, especially as an auxiliary; aiding, strengthening, confirming, etc., in a secondary or subordinate way: as, collateral aid; collateral security (see below); collateral evidence

You may be asking, how is this relevant? Oh... just you wait, you are going to love this!

Traditionally when we hear the word, we think bank collateral. You risk something to get something else. A mortgage risks your house for money. A business loan risks your credit for capital...etc. Sound familiar? When you speak your mind, or ask for what you want, you're also risking something, are you not? That risk is scary, it's unknown, and there could be consequences. But, just like a mortgage or starting a new business, that risk could also have tremendous reward.

The next way we often consider collateral is in the subordinate sense. Something that happens indirectly or secondarily to another. Think: Collateral damage. We've all heard that term, but what does it mean exactly? It means that every action we take could indirectly impact other seemingly unrelated things. (See butterfly effect.) Typically collateral in this way is viewed from a negative lens, but it can also work in the opposite way.

This is "collateral reward":

1. **You call someone out respectfully on their BS, and they level up** — That tough conversation you were dreading? It sparks real change. They stop making excuses, take responsibility, and everyone—including you—benefits from a stronger, more accountable relationship.
2. **You step up and address the elephant in the room, and suddenly the team's on fire** — Your courage to speak up breaks through the awkward silence, and now your team is operating at 110%. You've turned a dysfunctional mess into a powerhouse of efficiency and collaboration.
3. **You set clear boundaries, and suddenly people respect your time** — No more last-minute requests or overstepped limits. By standing your ground and communicating directly, you've trained people to value your time and energy—and now you can focus on what really matters.
4. **You offer some real talk to a friend spiraling out of control, and they snap out of it** — Your brutal honesty isn't easy, but it's the lifeline they didn't know they needed. Suddenly, they're back on track, making smarter choices, and turning their life around. The ripple effect? Everyone in their orbit benefits too.
5. **You challenge the status quo at work, and suddenly, you're the catalyst for change** — That thing no one wanted to talk about? You faced it head-on. Now the whole company culture is shifting, and guess what? Productivity, morale, and retention are all climbing.
6. **You genuinely listen to someone feeling invisible, and now they're unstoppable** — That one moment of real connection you offered? It boosts their confidence, and now they're kicking ass, not just in that moment but in everything they touch moving forward.
7. **You refuse to let something slide, and now everything improves** — By addressing a problem instead of ignoring it,

you've set a higher standard, not just for that situation, but for every interaction moving forward. Now everyone knows where the bar is, and they're stepping up.

I would like to propose a very different way of looking at collateral and what that can mean for you within the context of conversations and relationships.

The unseen negotiation in every conversation

Every single conversation you have is a negotiation. Whether you realize it or not, you're putting something on the table every time you open your mouth. Sometimes, it's obvious. You want something, you ask for it. "Hey, pass the salt." Done. But what about the conversations where you don't even know what the hell you want? Maybe you're looking for reassurance, respect, or just some damn attention. You feel it, but you can't quite put it into words. Welcome to the mess that is human communication. We're terrible at figuring out what we need, and even worse at asking for it.

Even when you don't know what you want, there's still collateral in play. You're giving something, whether it's vulnerability, time, or energy. You're investing, and the real question is: what are you getting back? You've been there. You need to have a conversation, but you have no clue where to start. You don't know what to say, or even what the hell you're trying to achieve. So, what do you do? **You avoid it.** You sweep it under the rug, thinking it'll fix itself. (Spoiler Alert: It won't.) Avoidance is a one-way ticket to nowhere.

Collateral means you've gotta give to get. You walk into a bank for a mortgage — you want the house, but what's the down payment? How much interest are you willing to pay? Can you handle the monthly cost? The same rules apply to communication. What are you willing to give up to get what you need? Are you ready to put yourself out there?

But, what if both sides are flying blind? What if neither of you knows exactly what's on the table? These are the conversations that trip us up the most. The ones where you feel something's off, but you're not sure what, and neither is the other person. Most people bail at this point because they don't want to deal with the mess. That's a mistake. If you don't know what you need, you still have to show up. The act of engaging is your collateral. You might not know exactly what you want to get out of the conversation, but you need to be willing to put something in.

Vulnerability is your down payment. **Patience** is the interest. And **honesty?** That's the full collateral you're putting on the line.

If you're sitting around waiting for all the "terms" to be perfectly clear before you have the conversation, you'll be waiting forever. The right moment? **It doesn't exist.** You've gotta start the damn conversation and figure it out as you go. What are you willing to give? How much are you ready to risk? Are you prepared to show up vulnerable and take a hit if necessary? Because real communication requires that you give something — and sometimes it's messy as hell.

Stop avoiding the hard conversations. You've got to engage, negotiate, and be willing to take risks. If you don't ask, you don't get. If you don't give, you don't get. It's that simple.

Social capital is your secret weapon (Use It!)

Taking the collateral analogy one step further, Social capital is the hidden currency you didn't even know you were earning (or squandering) every moment of every day. And the best part? You get to decide how much of it you bank—or blow—through the words you say and the actions you take. Think of it like an emotional bank account with every person in your life. Each interaction is either a deposit (trust, goodwill, and connection) or a withdrawal (distrust, distance, and irritation). So, it's up to you whether you're building up equity or heading straight for a bankruptcy of relationships.

You want people to have your back when you need it, right? Good. Then start investing **NOW**.

Social capital isn't just this fluffy "networking" term you've heard at business conferences. It's a powerful, behind-the-scenes force that makes sh*t happen when you need it most. The difference between getting that promotion, pulling together a winning team, or rallying support for a crazy idea comes down to how much trust and respect you've built. And if you think you can fake it 'til you make it here, think again.

Here's how it works:

- **Deposits**: Every time you show up, speak honestly, respect someone's time, or make them feel valued, you're depositing into your social capital account. This isn't some transactional BS—it's about proving, through action, that people can rely on you.
    - **Example**: You help a colleague with a project, even when it's not your job. You follow through on your promises. You remember someone's damn birthday, for crying out loud. These things seem small, but over time, they build a MASSIVE reserve of trust.
- **Debits**: And don't think for a second you can skate by on one good deed. When you **screw up**—like ignoring someone, taking credit for their idea, or ghosting them when they need

you—you're making a withdrawal. Too many withdrawals, and suddenly, no one wants to lend you their time or effort.

  - **Example**: You've been "too busy" to check in with a friend, and now, when you need a favor, they're suddenly MIA. Or, you said you would do something and didn't come through on your end of the deal. Newsflash: You burned your social capital, and now you're reaping the consequences.

- **Withdrawals:** Withdrawals are when you **cash in** on the social capital you've built. But, this isn't a free pass to start burning reserves. Withdrawals are for when you've earned enough trust and goodwill through consistent deposits, and now it's time to use that credit to ask for something you need. It's like calling in a favor, but without the guilt, because people **want** to help you since you've earned it.

  - **Example:** You need someone to cover for you at work because you're double-booked, but you've been solid for them so many times before. Or you're running late to a meeting, but no one bats an eye because you've always been reliable. This is your moment of trust payoff—people are willing to go the extra mile for you because you've built a freaking fortress of goodwill.

However, you can't keep cashing in if you're not replenishing that account. Withdrawals need to be **strategic**—you can't expect others to keep giving if you're not still making those consistent deposits. Keep the balance right, and people will show up for you every time.

Think of social capital as your strategic safety net. People are more likely to go to bat for you, give you honest feedback, and stick with you through tough times if you've been investing in that relationship. They don't do it because they owe you; they do it because they want to. They TRUST you. The truth? **The world doesn't owe you sh*t.**

If you want people to help you, listen to you, and support you, you've gotta earn it. And you earn it by consistently showing up as someone who gives a damn.

In your career, do you want that raise, that promotion, or new opportunity? It's not going to be based solely on your performance; it's about how much social capital you've built with your team and bosses. Are you seen as someone people trust, who delivers value, and who cares about the people around you? If not, you're just another cog in the corporate machine. In your personal relationships, do you want a solid network of friends, colleagues, and mentors? Invest in them. It's not enough to just show up when you need something. **Be there for them first**, and trust me, when the time comes, they'll be there for you too.

Say What You Mean, and Mean What You Say: No one has time for vague BS. Every time you speak clearly and follow through, you're depositing into your social capital account. Every time you flake out or dodge responsibility, you're making a withdrawal.

Give Before You Take: You want people to have your back? Have theirs first. Offer help, advice, or support without expecting anything in return. That's how you build goodwill that lasts. It's not about keeping score—it's about showing you care consistently.

Be Consistent: Building social capital isn't a one-time event. It's not enough to be a hero once and then coast. You need to be **reliable AF** over time. People remember how you show up consistently, not how you showed up that one time you needed something.

Own Your Mistakes: If you screw up (and you will), the best way to minimize that withdrawal is to **own your sh*t**. Apologize, fix it, and move forward. People respect someone who takes responsibility, and that kind of transparency can even become a deposit when handled right.

Alright, so now you've got the concept of collateral down—you know what it takes to build up your social capital and how to avoid draining it dry. But even if you've got a fat stack of social currency, it's not worth much if you don't know **how** and **when** to use it. That's where coordination comes into play.

You've got all the right cards in your hand, but it's not just about throwing them on the table and hoping for the best. It's about knowing who you're playing with, when to push, when to pull back, and how to strategically use what you've built to influence the right people at the right time. Coordination is about identifying your players, understanding what drives them, and figuring out the best way to navigate each individual to get the results you want. You've got the collateral. Now let's talk about how to cash it in with precision and purpose.

Coordination:

Coordination isn't just about organizing schedules or syncing calendars—it's about getting tactical with how you communicate and who you communicate with. Most people think that one-size-fits-all communication is going to work, but that couldn't be further from the truth. Think of Coordination as your personal strategy for making sure you're using **the right words, with the right people, at the right time.** Whether it's a project team, a relationship, or a massive group of stakeholders, you need to know who you're dealing with. And unfortunately, not everyone gets the same playbook.

In any situation, you're typically going to encounter three key types of people. Understanding who you're dealing with—and coordinating your communication accordingly—makes all the difference between resistance and change.

The Three Types of Stakeholders:

- **Boosters** (The Champions): Full of energy, pushing you forward, and always looking for ways to accelerate the mission.
- **Balancers** (The Fence Sitters): These folks keep things neutral, making decisions based on who has the most compelling argument.
- **Boulders** (The Nay-Sayers): They weigh things down, resisting change and progress at every opportunity.

1. **Boosters** (aka Champions)

These are your **ride-or-die** supporters. They've got your back, they see the vision, and they're ready to go to war for you. They don't need much convincing; they're already bought in. What do they need? Regular updates, clarity, and some fuel for their fire. The Gladiators are motivated by progress, transparency, and a sense of ownership in the outcome. So give them what they want: insider information, responsibility, and trust. Your job here? Keep them informed, keep them engaged, and, most importantly, let them feel like they're making an impact.

Collateral for Boosters: Show them the long-term benefits, give them the blueprint, and let them in on the decision-making process. Feed their ambition with ownership and responsibility.

Action Plan: Be transparent and empowering. Boosters thrive on being in the loop and knowing their contributions matter. Don't micromanage them, but don't leave them in the dark either.

2. Balancers (aka Fence sitters)

These folks are the hardest to pin down. They're not against you, but they're not jumping up and down to help either. They're in this for one reason: **stability**. These are your "I'll go with the flow, as long as it doesn't rock my boat" people. They're motivated by predictability, and they hate unnecessary drama. These people are key to winning over because they're the ones who can tip the balance. When things go smoothly, they'll follow the Gladiators. When things get messy, they might lean towards the Nay-Sayers.

Collateral for Balancers: Give them certainty. Show them how their day-to-day won't be disrupted—or better yet, how it'll improve. Your message to them? "Here's what's happening, here's how it affects you, and here's why you shouldn't worry."

Action Plan: Be calm, confident, and consistent. The Middle Grounders don't need to feel like heroes—they just need to feel secure. Make it clear that you're not messing with their comfort zone.

3. Boulders (aka Nay-sayers)

Ah, the Nay-Sayers. The ones completely set in stone that you run into over and over again. These folks are your critics, doubters, and the ones who shoot holes in every idea. But the truth it that **they're not always wrong.** These are the people who are going to poke at your plans, raise red flags, and ask a ton of questions. What drives them? Fear, skepticism, and control. They're worried about change, and their default mode is defensive.

The temptation here is to ignore them, but that's a mistake. Instead, use their critiques as a litmus test. If you can answer their questions, your plan probably holds water. And if you can't, they might have found a real gap you need to address. But—**don't get sucked into their negativity**. Their goal is control, so if you can acknowledge their concerns and **give them power** without succumbing to the darkness, you both can win.

Collateral for Boulders: Give them agency. Include them in the discovery and ideation process. Show them the **facts**. They need data, backup plans, and reassurance that the ship isn't about to sink. You're not here to win them over emotionally (but that wouldn't hurt)—you're here to give them a sense of control and proof that you're going to do what you say you're going to do.

Action Plan: Be firm but fair. Respect their need for answers, but manage the narrative and conversation. You'll need to handle Nay-Sayers with confidence—stand your ground, answer their questions, give them agency to be heard but don't let their fear pull you off course.

Coordination ties it all together understanding that these three types of people—the Gladiators, the Middle Grounders, and the Anchors—need completely different approaches. If you try to use the same collateral and communication style with all of them, **you're going to fail.**

- **Boosters?** They need inspiration and a front-row seat to your progress.
- **Balancers?** They need reassurance and consistency to keep them from jumping ship.

- **Blockers?** They need facts, logic, and to be heard, but the negativity cannot indulged.

Coordination is about knowing who to engage and how to engage them. It's a game of chess—strategizing your moves based on your stakeholders' unique motivations and needs. But, even the best strategies fall apart if you don't show up ***consistently***. You can't just coordinate the right message to the right people once and call it a day. Consistency is what turns your one-time efforts into long-term wins. It's what keeps the trust, momentum, and results flowing. Whether you're celebrating with the Boosters, reassuring the Fence-Sitters, or keeping the Anchors in check—consistent action is the warm blanket that keeps everyone. One great move won't win the game. It's the *follow-through* that turns your strategy into success.

Consistency:

You can have all the great ideas, all the clever one-liners, and all the charm in the world, but if you're not **consistent**, none of it matters. People don't trust someone who shows up once in a while, says something brilliant, and then disappears into the ether. They trust the people who **show up every damn day**, deliver on what they say, and follow through. Don't just talk about it, be about it.

What makes a person credible? It's not their one-off grand gesture or that one time they said something that really hit home. **Credibility is built on a foundation of repeated action.** If you're not backing up your words with action—and doing it over and over again—you might as well not say anything at all. Consistency is hard. It's not sexy. It's not glamorous. But it's the difference between being someone people can rely on, and being someone they roll their eyes at. You can't just swoop in, drop a nugget of wisdom, and expect people to change their entire worldview. They need to see you walk the walk. And they need to see it all the time.

Consistency = Reliability = Trust
If you're not consistent, you're not reliable. And if you're not reliable, you're not trusted. End of story.

People want to know that you're the same person on a Tuesday morning as you are on a Friday night. They want to know that whether the stakes are high or low, you're going to show up the same way. Consistency builds trust, and trust is the backbone of any relationship, team, or project. **One act of inconsistency can undo months or years of solid work.** If you show up strong 99 times and flake out once? Guess what? People remember the flake. People have long memories when it comes to being let down, and it takes a lot longer to rebuild trust than to maintain it in the first place.

Consistency isn't just doing the same thing over and over again. That's called repetition, and it's boring. Consistency is about delivering the same level of commitment, energy, and clarity every time you engage. Whether you're having a tough conversation, giving feedback, or leading a project, people need to know that you mean what you say, and you'll back it up every time.

- **In communication**: If you say you're going to check in, then check in. If you're a straight shooter today, don't turn into a politician tomorrow. People should know what they're going to get from you, every single time.
- **In action**: If you promise to deliver by Friday, deliver by Friday. Not Saturday, not Monday—**Friday.** And if something goes sideways and you can't hit the mark, say so immediately. Don't leave people hanging. Own it.

- **In relationships**: Be the person who's present, whether it's an easy conversation or a hard one. Don't be someone who only shows up when things are going well. Show up when it's messy. Show up when it's uncomfortable. That's what builds trust.
- **In leadership**: Be clear about your expectations, and then keep those expectations consistent. People should never have to guess where you stand or what you want. They should know—because you've shown them, repeatedly.

A lot of people confuse consistency with being rigid. "But I need to be flexible!" you say. Look, flexibility doesn't mean you can't be consistent. You can adapt and pivot without losing your integrity. Consistency isn't about being stuck in your ways—it's about being dependable. When you say you're going to pivot, people trust that your reasons, because your track record gives them that trust in you. The difference? Inconsistent people change with the wind. They flip-flop based on who's in the room or what mood they're in. Consistent people can shift gears while still holding onto their values and commitments. That's flexibility with integrity, and people can **feel** the difference.

I'm going to let you in on a little secret: Consistency isn't exciting, but it works. It's not going to make headlines, but it's going to make progress. Being consistent isn't about showing off—it's about being the person people can count on. Every. Single. Time. And when people can count on you, you become unstoppable.

Think about your favorite brands. What keeps you coming back? It's probably not the one-off sale or that flashy commercial they ran a few months ago. It's because every time you interact with them, you know exactly what to expect—and they **deliver**. Now, imagine if you became that brand. The person everyone knows they can trust. The one who does what they say they're going to do. The brand that's not just a fad but a lasting legacy.

People know what I'm going to say before I say it. So much so that I have people throw out my catch phrases in the middle of a conversation before I have a chance to say them: (If you have others, I would love to hear them!)

- "Words Matter!"
- "The answer to the question you never ask is always no."
- "Nothing changes if you do nothing."
- And when I'm just out of words… "I got nothing."

If you're going to be someone who practices Kind Transparency, you better be consistent about it. People need to know that you're not just "kind" and "transparent" when it's convenient. They need to know you're going to show up with that same level of honesty and authenticity whether they're loving what you're saying or squirming in their seat. Inconsistent transparency is worse than no transparency at all. Why? Because when you're inconsistent, people don't trust that what you're saying is the whole truth. They start second-guessing, they start reading between the lines—and once that happens, you've lost them.

So here's a challenge for you: Be the person who shows up the same way, day in and day out. Be the person who follows through, who delivers, and who stands by their word. Be the person people can rely on—not just when things are good, but when things are hard. At the end of the day, your reputation is built on what you do repeatedly, not what you do occasionally. If you want to be known as someone who can be trusted—prove it, over and over again. It's not glamorous. It's not flashy. But it's how you build something that lasts. Consistency is the foundation for everything. Without it, you're just another person who says a lot but delivers nothing.

Consistency in your language is **non-negotiable.** If your words shift depending on the situation, mood, or who you're talking to, people won't know how to interpret or trust what you're saying. Here's the brutal truth: when you're inconsistent in your communication, it forces people to play mind games—they'll spend more time decoding your message, questioning your motives, and second-guessing your intentions. The result? Nothing gets done, and trust takes a nosedive. But if your words *always* mean what you say—every single time—people stop second-guessing you. When your message is consistent, clear, and reliable, your audience can focus on what matters: the feedback or direction you're giving, not figuring out what you *really* mean. It's simple: consistent language builds trust and clarity. Without it, you're just creating confusion and wasting everyone's time.

In addition to saying what you mean, there is also a time and place to say it. There's never a wrong time to say how you feel, but there are certainly inopportune times. There's a reason why at weddings they ask - "Should anyone present know of any reason that this couple should not be joined in holy matrimony, speak now or forever hold your peace." If there was ever a time to say it, it's then (or well before), because more often than not, once a moment passes, it's gone. Of course you can revisit it, but the impact of the message isn't the same as if it were said immediately.

Think about how you train a new puppy. When the puppy has an accident, you address and correct it immediately. You redirect the puppy's behaviors through modeling, guidance and positive reinforcement. You wouldn't watch a puppy pee on the floor, get mad, stew about it, then explode and yell at it 4 hours later. (I hope you wouldn't) The puppy wouldn't understand. There is no longer correlation between the action and the response. It's the same way with humans. When you communicate and address things in the moment, you allow for immediate correlations, better understanding, and reduced escalation over time. If you stay quiet time after time when someone else is impacting you, you degrade the impact of the potential resolution, and eventually the relationship.

Back to our puppy. As important as the right timing is in communication, you have to back it up with consistency. If you scold it for peeing on the carpet today, you must do it tomorrow as well. Otherwise, it's getting mixed signals. Similarly, if you don't say anything and allow a behavior over time, but out of nowhere get upset about it, that's just as bad. People can't read your mind; they can only read your actions.

4 C's (Communication, Collateral, Coordination, and Consistency) aren't about being perfect or having all the answers. It's about showing up, speaking clearly, and sticking to your word. If people have to guess what you mean or wonder if you're full of crap, they're

not going to trust you. So, stop making things harder than they need to be. Say what you mean, mean what you say, and keep it consistent.

Influence doesn't come from having it all figured out—it comes from being intentional with every word and action. You don't need to be flawless; you just need to be real and reliable. Own your message, back it up with action, and stop dancing around the hard stuff. Show up. Be direct. Cut the crap. That's how you lead with Kind Transparency.

3

The Human Blueprint

As leaders (and stewards of humanity) we must understand that people are not simply what you see before you. They cannot be defined by who they are in a singular moment or action. Every person you meet has a different combination of experiences and biological predispositions that shape the paradigm, or lens from which they view the world through. **(Even you!)** This is the second, and quite possibly the most important concept you must grasp in your journey toward human connection.

> Did you think we were going to jump straight into the People Magic? Sorry, you gotta put in some work first!

In the chaos of our daily lives, it's easy to overlook one simple truth: every person we encounter, whether in the office or within our personal circles, carries with them a myriad of experiences that have sculpted their unique existence. This unique combination of encounters, challenges, and triumphs serves as the architect of their personality and beliefs, creating a one-of-a-kind perspective on the world.

But how often do we pause to ponder these life experiences and what they truly mean for those we interact with? In the mad rush of our routines, we may have no more than a cursory understanding of the people surrounding us. We see coworkers, friends, and acquaintances, but do we truly know them? Do we grasp the depth of their experiences or the battles they face beyond our shared interactions?

When you consider the individuals within your sphere, take a moment to reflect:
- You may notice that a colleague, who always seems infallible, discreetly battles chronic migraines, making you realize how much they must endure to push through their day.
- Or the friendly parent at your child's school pickup that always seems so put together, might be going through a divorce, and is struggling to make it all happen.
- Maybe the neighbor who hyper focuses on their lawn is secretly grappling with financial challenges and uses this outlet to keep up appearances.

The truth is, everyone you meet has a story, and understanding those stories is the key to forging more meaningful connections.

In this chapter, we're diving into what makes people tick, the real stories behind the faces you see every day. We're not here to scratch the surface, we're going deep. We're talking about understanding where people come from, why they act the way they do, and how you can unlock empathy to build stronger, more authentic connections. Ready to get uncomfortable? Good. Because that's where the magic happens.

Now, let's talk about what I call the "People Blueprint." You're not just some random design thrown together by chance. You're the result of two forces constantly battling it out: **nature** and **nurture**. (FYI - I can see you rolling your eyes.) I know this concept is played out and absolutely beat to death, but there really is something behind it, and it's important for us to frame our work with this mindset. I promise to not make it to boring or fluffy, but I need you to get it.

Let's start with very cliche metaphor. Imagine you're a plot of land, full of potential, waiting to be built into something amazing. Nature? That's the blueprint you inherit. Nature is the foundational stuff. Your genetic hand-me-downs. It's the stuff you can't easily change, like the foundation of a house. In real life, these are things like your natural temperament, your innate talents, and even some of your quirks. This is the "ancestral home" that you're given, whether you like it or not.

Nurture? That's the builder, modifying, enhancing, and sometimes screwing with the original plans. And, this is where things get interesting. Nurture is the life you live, the people you meet, the drama, the wins, the losses—all of it is shaping and reshaping who you are. Nurture is the builder that comes in with a hammer, knocking down walls, adding new rooms, and visually reshaping the character of the house. Your life experiences? They're the interior designers, shaping the structure of your personality.

Your *People Blueprint* is a mash-up of these forces, working together (or against each other) to build who you are. When you understand this, not only about yourself but about everyone else around you, it changes the prospective. You start seeing people as more than just their surface-level actions and attitudes. You start recognizing that behind every person is a history, a set of experiences, and a sh*t ton of unfinished construction that makes them act the way they do. So, as we keep digging into this chapter, let's break down how these pieces (nature and nurture) work together to shape the people in your life. Because once you can read that blueprint? You can finally start building real, honest connections.

At the end of the day, we're all "under construction." It never really ends. We're all evolving, learning, and tweaking the designs as we go.

So, don't get hung up on where you started. Focus on where you're going, and how you can build something even better, brick by brick. Nature really is like the family estate passed down to us, complete with weird wallpaper and furniture that nobody really asked for. (And yes, mine was probably covered in glitter wallpaper and had a broken front door that never quite closed right.) But we're talking about **your** foundation and of those around you, not just any old fixer upper.

Alright, I know what you're thinking—*"Another building metaphor? Really? I didn't sign up for a home improvement show."* Trust me, I get it. At this point, we've talked more about home remodeling than HGTV on a Tuesday night. But hang in there—I promise I won't ask you to install crown molding or pick out a back splash. (yet...)

nature

n.

1. *the fundamental or inherent qualities of something. See essence.*

OK let's focus.

We've been throwing around a lot of boring fluffy stuff in this chapter. But, there is a reason. The more we understand **why** we are the way we are (like, really understand it) the easier it becomes to cut other people some slack for their own weirdness. When you start recognizing that your own quirks and habits are a product of that ugly crap you inherited, you start realizing that **everyone** has their own sh*t they're dealing with, too.

And you know what? Once you get that, you stop seeing people as just annoying or difficult. Instead, you start thinking, "Oh, I know their *why*." That doesn't mean you have to love it, but it sure as hell makes it easier to connect with them. When you can see *why* someone acts the way they do, it's like having a cheat code to understand them better. And when you understand that context, you can relate in a way that actually makes sense to both of you, without all the drama and misunderstandings. So yes, knowing your own blueprint is important, but understanding other people's? That is where the magic happens. That's where connection stops being a guessing game and starts being real.

So, now that you've got the bigger picture on understanding the "why" behind people's behaviors, let's take it down a notch and dive into something more concrete. Because theory is great, but unless you see how it plays out in real life, it's just noise. Knowing someone's underlying temperaments is half the battle, but it's what happens when those reactions hit the real world that matters. So, let's shift gears (forgive the foreshadowing) and make this a bit more relatable. At this point, to give you a break, we're going to move on to a slightly different but equally cliche metaphor.

You're welcome.

Imagine this scenario: Instead of people, we're now all cars. You've got all these new parts that have to work together to keep things running smoothly. But, what kind of car are you? Just like in real life, not all cars are created equal. Some people are rolling around as reliable, no-frills daily drivers. Others are stuck with beaters that seem to break down at every stoplight. And then, there's that person who ends up as a race car. Lucky, right? Well… not so fast.

When we're talking race cars, we're talking about something that's designed to go *fast*. It's got a finely-tuned engine that's built to handle the pressure and the constant acceleration. In the short term, that's great. You've got the power to sprint, react quickly, and keep up in intense situations. Your sympathetic nervous system (the part responsible for your "fight or flight" response) is always ready, foot on the gas. It's what makes you respond immediately to stress, giving you that jolt of adrenaline to get through the moment.

But, the problem is, what happens when the throttle gets stuck? What happens when that race car is constantly revving, and there's no off switch? Imagine your engine just roaring at top speed non-stop. You're burning through fuel like crazy, your engine's working overtime, and sooner or later, you're going to blow a gasket. No one, and I mean no one, can run like that forever. (Spoiler Alert) That's exactly what's happening when you're in a constant state of stress, anxiety, or overdrive. Under the surface, your sympathetic nervous system, that handy little system that's supposed to get you out of danger, is always switched on. You're stuck in "fight or flight," even when there's no danger around. The result? Your body starts to wear down, your mental and emotional reserves get depleted, and you're well on your way to burnout.

Just like a race car can't run at full throttle without pit stops, your body can't handle the constant revving. Eventually, the engine overheats, parts start to break down, and if you don't take care of it? It'll be out of commission entirely. Same for humans. Chronic anxiety, exhaustion, and eventually burnout. It's your body's way of screaming, "Enough already!"

> Now, I'm the last person to lecture anyone on this, but I can confirm that you have to take a break from time to time.

Logically, you might be thinking, "Wouldn't that be a gift? Wouldn't being able to run on all cylinders mean I can do more, achieve more?" And sure, there are short term benefits to having that kind of edge – quick reactions, heightened alertness, the ability to handle high-pressure situations. But here's the thing: if you don't learn how to manage it, that gift will turn into a burden faster than you can say "check engine light."

And it's important to remember that running at full speed all the time affects more than just your physical state. It messes with you psychologically too. Constant stress can alter the way you think and react. It makes you more reactive, more likely to snap, and less able to slow down and think things through. That "high-performance" brain of yours? It's great for sprints, but not for the marathon of life. You'll find yourself worn out, mentally scattered, and struggling to focus on anything beyond the next crisis.

This, for me, sometimes looks like jumping and grabbing the door in the car when my husband is driving because my mind is constantly envisioning **every** possible scenario and calculating the likelihood of it happening.

"Someone is turning in front of us with too little time!"

FLINCH!

"They aren't slowing down fast enough at the red light!"

JUMP!

"That guy is eating a sandwich and started drifting!"

CLENCHES PEARLS!

Sorry babe

If we're keeping on the path of completely random metaphors, let's look at one that's on the complete opposite spectrum of the race car. Picture a totally relaxed, orange tabby cat lounging in the sun. (His name is Charlie.) He wakes up as you pass him and starts a litany of meows indicating he wants food, pets, and to sit on your laptop keyboard. He also doesn't seem to mind you desperately trying to get him out of your favorite chair. But, what's really going on with Charlie?

His laid-back feline attitude might remind you of your overly-chill buddy from high school, and you'd be right, because they have a lot more in common than you'd think. That thing being something called "low cortical activation". It's basically a fancy way of saying your brain isn't firing on all cylinders all the time. For some people, their baseline state is naturally more relaxed. Less stress, less overthinking, just *less* in general. When you have low cortical activation, your brain isn't overloading you with stimuli or stress responses. This is why people with low activation tend to stay calm even when the world's on fire. They don't feel the need to react immediately or get worked up because, internally, their system isn't demanding it. They're not flooded with adrenaline or racing thoughts. Think of it as the brain's "chill mode."

Now, let's circle back to Charlie. He's lounging in the sun, sprawled out without a care in the world. When you walk by, he slowly wakes up, shoots you a lazy meow, maybe stretches, and then demands some attention (or food – because he's a cat). He doesn't bolt or get startled. He's not anxious. He's just... Charlie. That's low cortical activation in action. He's operating at a calm, low-level baseline, completely unbothered by the world around him.

There is another level to this that makes it more interesting too. This low activation doesn't just mean someone stays calm. It can also lead to impulsivity. Because they're not overwhelmed by stimuli, they often act on immediate desires without much thought. Look at Charlie again: he sees your chair, wants it, and suddenly, he's in it. He doesn't care that it's your chair, or that you were about to sit there. His brain isn't overthinking it, he's just going for what he wants.

Same for humans. That calm, low-key demeanor can lead to quick, impulsive decisions because there's no internal chaos slowing them down or making them second-guess everything. They see something they want and they go for it. They're often more extroverted because they're not bogged down by overthinking. (I can't relate...) They're willing to dive headfirst into social situations or opportunities without getting wrapped up in all the "what if's" that might hold someone else back.

Have you ever wondered why your extroverted, spontaneous friend can stay calm in stressful situations but also make snap decisions with the confidence of a rock star? That's probably the low cortical activation. They're wired to stay cool under pressure, but also jump into action when they feel like it – and just like Charlie, they're probably not worried about taking over your favorite chair. Understanding this about people (and your pets) can go a long way in knowing how to communicate and connect with them. They're not necessarily being careless; they're just wired differently.

So, what's the bottom line? Your inner wiring (nature) is what shapes your quirks and traits. It's like being handed a hard drive by Mother Nature herself. You're kinda stuck with it, but knowing your hardware helps you navigate which software you should install throughout your life. It's all about understanding yourself and embracing your unique coding.

But wait, there's more!

nurture

1. *n. the totality of environmental factors that influence the development and behavior of a person, particularly sociocultural and ecological factors such as family attributes, parental child-rearing practices, and economic status. Compare nature. See also nature–nurture.*

Who we are isn't just some pre-programmed biological blueprint we're born with. Sure, genetics gave us a starting point, but everything else? That's all on you and what life's thrown at you.

Every single situation, failure, triumph, embarrassing moment, success, and, most importantly, how you *decide* to interpret and process them. You are not the cards you've been dealt, but you are 100% responsible for how you play them. Period. Life doesn't care if you're having a good day, a bad day, or an "I spilled coffee on my white shirt in the middle of a meeting" day. It's going to throw some major curve balls, sometimes good, often bad, and occasionally, downright ugly. But, it's not the event itself that shapes you, but how you react to it.

Consider this: two people can go through the exact same train wreck of a situation and come out completely different on the other side. Why? Two reasons actually. The first goes back to nature. Some people are naturally better equipped to manage stress and cope with difficult situations. Genetic predispositions play a large part in how we experience the world. Everyone has unique triggers that bring out these natural tendencies, even if we work hard to suppress them. Fear, anger, depression, and avoidance—these are some seriously heavy hitters when it comes to reactions. Everyone has this capacity for reaction inside of them, just at varying levels. Some people are drowning in it; others barely have a toe in the water. It's just the way we're wired, and it's crucial to understand that we don't all show up to the game with the same playbook. Some people can rise above the chaos like it's no big deal, while others are barely keeping their head above water. And guess what? That's okay.

This is one of the biggest takeaways I want you to get: *not everyone is going to be on your level.* You might be out here thinking, "I'm crushing this. Why can't they just figure it out?" But the hard truth is, everyone's walking a different path, with different baggage, and at their own pace. You can't expect them to move through their challenges at the same speed you do. Some people take longer to process their anger, to push through their fear, or to climb out of their depressive fog. Your job? It's not to judge them for that. It's to meet them where they're at.

Everyone's paradigm is different.

You're looking at life through your lens, but they've got their own lens too. Their history, their trauma, their experiences—all of that stuff adds up to create their own personal paradigm, and it's not the same as yours. You might be able to brush off a failure, and they might get knocked on their a$$ by the same thing. You might bounce back from criticism, and they might spiral into self-doubt. It doesn't mean they're broken, and it doesn't mean you're better. It just means they're working from a different set of circumstances.

So, what do you do about it? You meet them where they are. You don't drag them up to your level and expect them to perform; you get down into the trenches with them and help them figure out what they need to be able to climb out. This is where empathy comes into play. You've got to look at their situation, see the obstacles they're facing, and realize that they might need different tools than you do.

The goal isn't to drag people along on your growth journey like they're dead weight. The goal is to help them find the tools that work for *them*. What works for you might not work for them. You can't just throw a self-help book at them and expect them to have the same "aha" moment you did. Maybe they need to learn how to manage their fear differently. Maybe they need to develop a habit that helps them process anger instead of bottling it up. Maybe avoidance has been their safety net for so long, they don't know any other way to deal. It's about helping them create *their* toolkit, not handing over yours and hoping for the best.

Everyone's capable, but not everyone's ready.

The second reason why two people can go through an experience and come out differently is that Everyone is *capable* of growth, but not everyone is ready for it. That doesn't make them weak; it just makes them human. They might not be ready to let go of their fear or anger. They might not even see that they're avoiding the hard stuff. You can't force them to "get it" right now. All you can do is support them when they're ready, help them find their way, and be patient.

At the end of the day, it's not about how fast you can grow. It's about making the choice to grow at all, even if it's just inching forward. So, the next time you're dealing with someone who's not "on your level," take a step back and remember: They're not on *your* level, because they're on *theirs*. Meet them there, and help them figure out how to move forward in their own way, at their own pace. Because in the end, it's not about dragging people up to where you are. It's about creating a world where we all rise together. One step at a time.

The caveat to this though, is that people need to make the active decision that they want to keep climbing. We all get to pick the kind of people we're going to be. We can either step up and face the crap head-on, or we sit down and let it swallow us whole. We make that choice. Every. Damn. Time.

This isn't just about the big stuff.

Sure, it's easy to focus on the major life-altering events. You know, the "my whole life fell apart" kind of stuff. But, the big moments aren't the only things shaping you. Nope, it's all the little crap too. The day-to-day irritations, the mundane BS, the minor inconveniences that add up and silently mold who you are just as much, if not more.

Ever had that one coworker who just wears on your nerves? You know the one. Every office has one. They talk too much, ignore deadlines, and somehow *always* manage to dump their work on you. So what are you going to do? Let it ruin your day? Let it fester until you blow up, or worse, passive-aggressively lose your mind in a thousand small ways? Yeah, that'll do wonders for your mental health. Or, here's an idea, shrug it off, deal with it directly, and keep it moving. One annoying coworker isn't worth wrecking your whole day over. Choose to react differently. Choose to be better.

Then there are those moments that feel like life's decided to sucker punch you right in the mouth. We've all had them. The job you didn't get, the relationship that went sideways, or the time you just flat-out failed at something you really cared about. These are the moments that test your grit. Do you come out the other side with a "victim badge" pinned to your chest, or do you come out swinging? Because here's the hard truth: It's not about pretending those tough moments didn't happen (they did, and they probably sucked.) It's about what you do *next*. Do you let that crap weigh you down like emotional baggage you drag into every interaction, or do you flip it on its head, learn from it, and come out stronger? Your past might be a weight, but you can use it as an anchor or a weapon. You get to decide which.

And it's not just about how you handle the heavy, soul-crushing stuff either. It's about how you manage the small fires life keeps lighting. Got stuck in traffic? Are you going to let it ruin your mood? Maybe your partner forgot to grab the milk *again*. Are you about to make that into a whole thing? It's not about the spilled milk (pun obviously intended). It's about how you choose to deal with it. You can let the small annoyances pile up and blow up later, or you can handle them for what they are, little hiccups that don't deserve to take up too much space in your head.

Life's going to hand you a lot of crap sandwiches. You can either take a bite and complain about the flavor, or you can toss it out and make yourself something better. Don't let your circumstances define you. Take control, even if it's just in how you respond. Because your reactions are the one thing you actually get to control. Choose to rise above, choose to grow, choose to keep it moving. That's Kind Transparency in action. You don't have to fake it, but you do have to face it.

OK, we've covered a ton of information so far, and maybe you're still like - "Why does any of this matter?" Well, let's take a moment to refocus and connect the dots. You want to be able to communicate better and say exactly what you want to (without being a jerk), right?

I thought so.

For the outcomes of your conversations to change, you must change. You need to be able to step back and holistically evaluate yourself as well as the person you are speaking to. Not just as who they are, standing in front of you in this moment, but as the collection of moments that brought this version of them to you. Then, and only then, can you determine the set of tools and levers that you'll need to open an authentic dialog.

4

Digging Deeper

"Chains of habit are too light to be felt until they are too heavy to be broken." - Warren Buffett

I'm just going to come out and say it, this is going to be another deep convo, touchy/feely chapter. Sorry, not sorry. Because this stuff *really* matters. Who you are isn't just some preset list of traits gifted to you by the universe. That was just the warm-up act. The real builder? It's all that crap life hurls at you, like a game of emotional dodge ball. (Remember nature?) But instead of those hits bouncing off, they stick around in three main ways: habits, conditioning, and trauma. Think of these three things as an unholy trio working together to either make you better or make you a hot mess. They don't hang out solo, they gang up and influence how you act, react, and show up in the world.

habit

1. a settled or regular tendency or practice, especially one that is hard to give up.

Habits are neither inherently good or bad, but in either case, those sneaky little bastards get created and somehow run our lives without us even noticing. They're the autopilot of our behavior, usually kicking in when we're too distracted, lazy, or overwhelmed to make conscious choices. Think of habits like those well-worn paths in the park that you just keep walking down because, honestly, it's easier than creating a new trail, even if it would lead you to someplace better. They help us get through the boring stuff in life, but what happens when they lead us down the wrong path?

Take stress as an example. Some people deal with stress by binge eating a bag of chips, while others might hit the gym to burn off steam. But on the more extreme side there are people, who in response to stress, pluck out their hair or eyebrows. (Seriously, it's a thing.) Habits aren't just random actions we repeat, they're coping mechanisms, reactions deeply ingrained in us from years of dodging life's punches. We fall back on them without even thinking, which is great when it's something productive. Not so much when it's... eyebrow-plucking.

But there is some good news: habits aren't permanent. You can tear down that well-worn path and create a shiny new one that doesn't lead straight to your doom. Sure, it takes some effort, but we can change them.

- You can switch from doom-scrolling Instagram to reading a damn book for once.

- You can stop endlessly hitting snooze and actually wake up when your alarm goes off like an adult.
- You can swap that fourth cup of coffee for some water before you dehydrate yourself into a raisin.
- You can stop ghosting friends and call them back before they assume you've joined a cult.

So how does this tie into Kind Transparency? I'm glad you asked. Ever avoided a hard conversation because you thought sweeping it under the rug was the easier option? How'd that work out for you? (Spoiler Alert: it didn't.) Everyone has swept issues under the rug, hoping they'll disappear. But instead of disappearing, more often than not, they fester and grow. The rug becomes moldy and starts to smell. You try to ignore it and pretend that everything is OK until it becomes so bad that other people start to notice. Something must be done. Trust me, we've all been there. I used to do it too—until I realized that making the habit of avoiding conflict was just creating a moldy mess I couldn't hide from anymore.

That's where a new habit comes in—open, honest dialogue. Imagine if instead of avoiding the tough conversations, we made it a habit to tackle them head-on. Yeah, it's uncomfortable, but it's also game-changing. Once you start practicing transparent communication, you stop reacting like a defensive jerk and start responding with empathy and understanding. And you'll be shocked at how much smoother things run when you actually deal with problems rather than hoping they'll just disappear.

In short, habits are the silent controllers of our lives. The key? Build the right ones. Replace your habit of avoidance with one of transparent communication. It's not just about talking more; it's about talking better—addressing conflict, discomfort, and those awkward moments with honesty. The end result? A world where real connection, empathy, and understanding thrive. So, yeah, I'm challenging you to break the bad habits, and build ones that actually serve you (and the people around you) better.

conditioning

1. the process of training or accustoming a person or animal to behave in a certain way or to accept certain circumstances.

Conditioning, in the context of human behavior, refers to the process by which individuals learn and adopt particular behaviors, responses, and thought patterns based on their experiences and interactions with their environment. It is a fundamental aspect of how humans adapt to their surroundings and develop a set of learned behaviors and responses over time.

There are two primary types of conditioning:

Classical Conditioning: This type of conditioning, famously studied by Ivan Pavlov, involves learning to associate a neutral stimulus with a specific response. For example, in Pavlov's experiments, he trained dogs to associate the sound of a bell with food, causing the dogs to salivate when they heard the bell ring, even when no food was present.

"Hey! I'm not a dog. How can I relate to this?"

In human terms, this might involve associating a particular place, person, or situation with a specific emotional response. What is your first thought when you're somewhere and unexpectedly smell rotten eggs? Gas leak, right? The utility companies have conditioned us to identify a very unique smell and then take a very specific action as a result. Another good example would be the lights and sirens on ambulances and police cars. What do you do if you hear an ambulance or see its lights? You pull over to the curb to allow it to pass. Sight, sound and smell are the key triggers in classical conditioning.

Operant Conditioning: This form of conditioning, explored by B.F. Skinner, focuses on the consequences of behavior. It involves learning through rewards and punishments. If a behavior leads to a favorable outcome, an individual is more likely to repeat that behavior. Conversely, if a behavior leads to an unfavorable outcome, they are less likely to repeat it. For example, an employee who receives more money for their hard work is more likely to continue putting in extra effort.

But, how does this play out in real life? Pizza Party anyone!?!? Why is it that when people go above and beyond, we always tell them we will reward them with food? "I owe you lunch!" - "Drinks are on me!" But, it can also be used with the opposite effect. How often do people that are great at their jobs get handed more work? So many managers, friends, spouses, and parents inadvertently (or purposefully) take an active action that says - "You're really good at this, instead of rewarding you, I'm going to give you more work." To make things worse, this extra work is often taken from someone else who could do it, but possibly not at the same quality. So, we've now effectively punished a high functioning motivated person for doing a good job, and conditioned a lower performer to do less and not try because they can get away with it.

Conditioning is one hell of a force in shaping human behavior. It's the reason you instinctively hit "ignore" when your phone rings, or why your mouth waters at the smell of bread even though you swore off carbs this week (don't worry, I won't tell). Every day, conditioning plays puppet master with our habits, attitudes, and knee-jerk reactions. Some of these learned behaviors are good, like brushing your teeth every morning without thinking. But really, some of them? Not so great. Like reaching for the phone and doom-scrolling the second you get a free minute, or rewarding yourself with junk food when you've had a "rough" day. *Queue the pizza party that no one actually asked for, but everyone shows up to.*

Conditioning is a result of what you've been through and repeated outcomes of those experiences. It's why some people get all starry-eyed when they hear a motivational speech, and others roll their eyes and wonder if there's a bar nearby. It's not random, it's a direct result of what's been drilled into your head over time. And while that conditioning might have gotten you through some tough situations, it doesn't always serve your best interests in the long run.

So why does this matter? Because once you recognize *how* and *why* you've been conditioned, you can stop letting it control your life. You don't have to keep reacting the same way just because you always have. Yes, you can *reprogram* your responses. Maybe you've been conditioned to avoid conflict at all costs, so now you ghost people instead of dealing with hard conversations. But guess what? You can unlearn that. You can condition yourself to face conflict head-on without feeling like the world is going to explode. One step, one small conversation at a time until new positive reinforcement is able to help you unlearn the previous conditioning.

All of that to say, you're not stuck with the automatic responses you've developed over the years. You can take control, and rewire the way you react to life's crap storms. But here's the catch: it takes *work*. It's not going to happen by accident. You need to identify the patterns that aren't serving you, and then make a conscious effort to replace them with ones that do. Condition yourself for success instead of sabotaging yourself with the same old habits.

So, next time you feel that knee-jerk reaction kicking in, stop for a second and ask yourself: *Is this habit or conditioning, is it actually helping me, or am I just on autopilot?* If it's not helping, it's time to hit the mental reset button and start reconditioning yourself for the better. Let's break the cycle!

Trauma

1. a deeply distressing or disturbing experience.

Alright, let's talk trauma. Real light subject matter here, I know. But if you've learned anything by this point in the book, it's that we have to talk about things, even when they're hard. Even if it's uncomfortable. Trauma isn't just a buzzword that gets tossed around for dramatic effect. (OK maybe sometimes.) It's typically some really terrible baggage that we didn't sign up for, but still have to carry around. I envision it to be a giant backpack full of rocks that you're lugging around with you through life, except they aren't rocks, they're actually sticks of dynamite and every once in a while one of them explodes.

Trauma's like that, creeping up on you when you least expect it. Impacting how you see the world, how you react, how you trust—or don't. Maybe you get jumpy at harmless things, or anxious for no reason. Or you shut down completely in certain situations, dodging things that remind you of that "bad stuff" from your past. In some ways, trauma turns you into your own personal alarm system, except the wiring's faulty, so it goes off unexpectedly, even when there's no actual fire.

Yeah, it sucks. But here's where I cut the pity party short. Yes, trauma's real, and it's heavy, and it's hard—but it's not the end of the story. You don't have to let it dictate your life forever. Trauma doesn't have to be your identity. It's like a broken bone that healed wrong. Yes, it might ache when the weather changes or when you overexert yourself, but with the right rehab, you can strengthen the muscles around it and keep moving. It'll always be part of you, but it doesn't have to hold you back. You can learn how to best live with it and start moving forward.

The process? It's basically rewiring your brain so that those old, explosive reactions don't control you anymore. It's recognizing that, yeah, you've been dealt a crappy hand, but that the story isn't over yet. You have to have the courage to take that backpack off one (explosive) rock at a time. The process takes work (therapy, self-reflection, leaning on the people who actually get it) but it's not impossible. And when you start to unpack all that stuff, you make room for growth, room for change, and room for healthier ways to handle all of life's BS.

And here's the thing, while you're doing the work on yourself, remember that the people around you have their own sh*t to unpack too. You never know what someone has been through or is still dragging around in their metaphorical backpack. It's easy to get frustrated or dismissive when someone's reactions seem over the top or completely out of left field, but that's when you have to pause and realize they're dealing with their own baseline of experience. If you take the time to actually get to know them, to build a foundation of trust, you give them the chance to share some piece of that baseline with you. Only then can real connection happen. When you stop assuming you know their story and actually invite them to tell it. It's not about forcing someone to open up; it's about creating a space where they feel safe enough to do so. Because until you understand what someone's carrying, you can't fully connect with them on a meaningful level. So yeah, do the work on yourself, but don't forget to extend that patience and understanding to others along the way. True connection comes from seeing past the surface.

And yeah, we could go on forever and dive into all the technical theories and labels that explain why people are the way they are, but if I'm being honest (and I usually am) understanding all of that isn't nearly as important as simply accepting that we all perceive the world in different ways. Once we have that as a common theme, we can start to see others for more than who they are in any given moment. The picture of a complex, multi-dimensional human being begins to unblur before us, allowing room for further discovery into the big picture.

Story Time

This concept of understanding people beyond face value isn't a new concept, but it is something that doesn't get discussed often enough. I wish I had learned this much earlier in life. It isn't something that we're born with.

As a teenager and early adult, I greatly struggled with communication. I had a very difficult time connecting with people. This may be an exaggeration, but it felt like I was completely incapable of understanding other people's feelings, reactions, and motivations. This made personal and professional relationships difficult or nearly impossible. Looking back now, I feel this was a combination of a lack of empathy and self-understanding.

I was a bright kid; I learned things quickly, did well in school, always looking for the next opportunity. I even skipped second grade. But where did that get me? That meant that I was younger than my peers, didn't relate to those around me, and spent more time with adults than children. Now, I had a wonderful childhood, don't get me wrong. But, as it was in those times (early 80's and 90's), my lack of social skill, empathy and connection was often explained away instead of nurtured.

> "That's just how she is…"
> "She's wise beyond her years."
> "She colors outside of the box."

In first grade, my mother was called to the school and was told that I should be tested for Asperger's (or what today would be classified as high functioning on the Autism spectrum). I don't know exactly what triggered the call, but I could venture a guess. I would often get bored at school, leave the classroom, and call home. I essentially did what was asked of me, then did whatever I wanted to do.

> (Yes, that is pretty much what I still do, but we're not talking about that right now!)

I remember her being livid. She told them absolutely NOT! But with a much more colorful vocabulary, in her very blunt way. I didn't really understand any of it at the time, but I do now. In the 90s, the stigma surrounding mental health issues cast a pervasive shadow over society. Mental health concerns were often shrouded in silence and shame, leading to a significant barrier for individuals seeking or needing help. Nobody wanted their kid to be "labeled". So, she did what she thought was best for me.

This happened to people all the time, and was almost always well intended. But what it did, looking back, was set me up for initial disappointment as an adult. I had an inflated sense of self-worth and paired that with an inability to see things from others' point of view. So, in any situation where things didn't go my way, I couldn't regulate. I had expectations and couldn't process when things turned out differently than I expected.

In high school, I was in the top of my class, without even trying. I barely even went to school in my senior year. Why? Because the people at school accommodated and perpetuated my behavior because they liked me. But, when I went to college, it was a completely different story. The playing field was leveled. I was no longer special, things were no longer easy, and I didn't have anyone there making excuses for me and my behavior.

Fast forward to early in my career. I remember so many situations that are just horrifying for me to think about now. This is an open apology to all my former managers who put up with me during this time!

- I would walk up to someone, or into their office and just stand there until they acknowledged me. Regardless of if they were talking to someone else or writing an email.
- I would propose an idea and wouldn't let it go, even after being told no many times.
- I would get involved in things that had nothing to do with me, sometimes at the detriment of my work.
- I would get overly frustrated by people and situations I didn't understand.

By now, I was self-aware enough to understand that I had a problem, but I had no idea how to change. (Did I have to change? Do I want to change? Surely this is their fault!) It's made further complex because some of these challenges are actually incredibly valuable tools if used properly. But, how do you know when to push and when to withdraw?

It was the same within my personal relationships, I did not consider the other person's feelings or understand why they wouldn't just accept my explanation of the situation. I wasn't communicating or setting clear expectations. I just expected other people to know my intentions.

So, throughout my late teens and early twenties, I spent a significant amount of my time and energy learning about psychology and human behavior. I would read any and everything I could get my hands on. (I still do.) Psychological theory, Leadership, Sales Training... And luckily, I have had so many amazing mentors throughout my career who were able to help me find the balance between when to push people and when to pull.

I tell you these things now, not to garner pity, or praise, but to show you that it's not just neuro-typical "Type A" people who become great leaders and communicators. Anyone can lead. Anyone can grow and improve. All it takes is caring, compassion and the will power to step across the party lines and see people for who they really are.

5

Why does it happen?

Alright, whew! That last part was emotional, let's lighten it up a bit in here!

As we know, communication isn't easy or comfortable, even for transparency enthusiasts like me. Why? Because we're all a bit imperfectly human. And being human comes with baggage. One of the things that takes up a ton of room in those bags is a very little thing called fear. That unsettling feeling that creeps in at the most inopportune times. It starts small but grows and grows and grows and compounds until we eventually face it (or don't). Whether we're afraid of how our words might be received, worried about overstepping our bounds, or unintentionally causing chaos. It's always there, just under the surface, lingering, waiting to come out and prevent us from moving forward.

Possibly worse than fear, are assumptions. We often assume others understand us perfectly, forgetting that we're each walking around with our own unique dictionary of life experiences. We need a translator. Misunderstandings happen when we only speak our language without considering the language of the receiver. You wouldn't go to a foreign country, speak your language, and then get mad when the natives don't understand you. You would try to find a common ground, a shared vocabulary or visuals that would connect your words with the ideas and concepts you are trying to convey. When your tool set is limited, you find new tools.

> "I suppose it is tempting, if the only tool you have is a hammer, to treat everything as if it were a nail."
> — Abraham Maslow

Next, we must consider the factor of time. In our fast-paced world, it's like we're all sprinting through a never-ending marathon of to-dos. Schedules clash, messages get lost in the digital abyss, and suddenly, the window for meaningful conversation is narrower than ever. The constant pressure to keep up with the pace of modern life not only limits the time we have for dialogue but also distracts us, making it harder to fully engage and connect with others. (I'd explain more, but "I'm too busy...")

Lastly, but certainly not least, vulnerability, in terms of communication, acts as a double-edged sword. On the one hand, it offers an opportunity for genuine connection, as it invites others to see our authentic selves. However, it's also a precarious tightrope walk, as sharing your thoughts and feelings can feel like stepping onto a stage under a bright spotlight. You're exposing yourself to an audience that could include either your most supportive allies or your most harsh critics, amplifying the fear of judgment or rejection. This inherent risk often leads us to hesitate, holding back our true thoughts and emotions, and contributing to the difficulty of open and honest communication.

So, whether it's fear, assumptions, the crazy pace of life, or the vulnerability of putting yourself out there, we all stumble. Every single one of us. But acknowledging our uncertainty, and realizing that everyone else feels the same way, is the first step towards that clear, authentic connection we're all after. It's all about embracing the messy, acknowledging the struggle, and working together to navigate the sometimes-bumpy road of communication with kindness, candor, and at least a little bit of humility.

Alright, I know we're getting a little esoteric here, but I assure you it's all part of the process. It's important that we define this level of understanding as we start peeling back the layers of complexity that make up this sh*tshow we call communication. I'm all about diving into the deep end, even when the waters get a bit murky, but you have to have a plan and some tools to help you get out.

Humans are amazingly skilled at crafting our own little bubbles of comfort. When faced with challenges, we tend to slide into these cozy retreats within ourselves. It's like building a fort out of blankets when the world outside gets too crazy. From our safe place, it's easy to start assuming that we know what others are thinking, and turning ourselves into amateur mind-readers. And, let's not forget how easily we then accept avoidance. If a conversation seems too daunting, we just retreat, sweep it under the rug, hoping the dust bunnies won't notice. (Oh, they notice. The dust bunnies remember!)

These little retreats often turn into echo chambers. Our assumptions echo back as facts, and avoidance becomes our default mode. It's like living in a bubble within a bubble, where our perspective gets narrower and narrower. We create these self-fulfilling prophecies, and false narratives. Suddenly, we're walled off from the very connection we were avoiding, and struggle to get back when we're finally ready to accept it.

I get it, these habits are like old friends that sometimes overstay their welcome. You let them in with good intentions, but eventually they are so intertwined into your daily life, it's hard to undo. But here's where the magic happens. Recognize the habits, acknowledge that they're not doing us any favors, and then taking a bold step outside of that comfort zone. It's when we break down that blanket fort and step outside into the rain, realizing that getting a little wet is a small price to pay for the clarity and growth that come with authentic communication. It's time to pop that bubble, and help others pop theirs, because life is richer when we all step out of our self-made prisons.

Still with me? Good, because we are going to dive even deeper into the human condition, and it's probably going to get a little weird...

I know by now you're not afraid to tackle the tough stuff; so, let's talk a little more about vulnerability. Most people talk about vulnerability as a weakness. But, I want to talk about leveraging vulnerability as a strength, because it is. We all know the potential downsides. There are potential downsides to everything. When used properly, it is a very powerful tool that overshadows the risk of its use.

Vulnerability is the heart and soul of real connection. It's when we open up, bare our thoughts, and say, "Hey world, here's the unfiltered version of me." But ugh, vulnerability can feel scary. We're conditioned to believe that showing our true selves (flaws, insecurities, and all) is like handing over a weapon that could be used against us. And that's not entirely wrong. That *could* happen. Remember, vulnerability is one of those things that gets used as collateral in communication. So, what do we usually do? We slap on that armor of self-preservation, hoping it'll shield us from judgment and hurt. But there's a big plot twist here. That armor doesn't just block out pain; it also barricades connection. Think of it as a door that slams shut, cutting off the flow of understanding, empathy, and growth. We trap ourselves in a fortress, where problems go unresolved, and relationships stagnate. It's like building a wall around our own hearts, and guess what? Hearts don't thrive in isolation – they thrive in circulation. (see what I did there?)

We must take that armor off, piece by piece. I'm not saying it's easy – vulnerability is a muscle that needs flexing. But when we muster the courage to say, "This is me, take it or leave it," we're not just opening ourselves up, we're tearing down the very walls that stand in the way of connection and healing. So, let's make vulnerability more mainstream and a companion in our daily lives. Let's use it as positive collateral. Because when we shed our armor, we create a space where true connection can flourish, and where problems get the chance to be heard, understood, and solved.

You're probably wondering, "Okay, all this talk about transparency and open communication sounds nice, but what am I supposed to *actually do* with this?" Great question. But before we get all action-packed, let's zoom out a little and talk about the *why*, because that's the core of all of this. Remember your "why" from earlier in the book? Why you're doing this, why you care about changing the way you communicate? Yeah, it's time to dig back into that. Regardless of your why, the way to get there is through clear open communication. There are two final points that I want to touch on in this chapter to help you in that goal:

1. The answer to the question you don't ask is always 'no'.
2. Say the thing.

Let me reiterate: The answer to the question you don't ask is always "no". Period. Hard stop.

- Want a raise? Didn't ask? NOPE.
- Want clarity on a problem? Stay silent? Good luck getting a solution.
- Want to connect with someone on a deeper level? But never ask them how they feel? You're missing the point entirely.

We sit on questions because we're afraid of rejection or we assume we already know the answer. But here's the thing: silence is your worst enemy. It's a guaranteed path to getting nowhere. You want better communication? Ask the damn question. I don't care if it's asking for clarification at work, diving into a tough conversation with a friend, or asking for that opportunity you've been eyeballing for months. ASK IT. Open your mouth, put it out there. That's the first step to progress.

In a world where we're so quick to text, tweet, or post a cryptic message, we've forgotten how to just *ask*. Stop standing on the sidelines waiting for someone to magically read your mind. If you want to make strides, it starts with one simple thing: ASKING. Don't get caught in the cycle of "what ifs" because you didn't have the guts to ask a question.

Here's where it gets tougher: **Say the thing you need to say.** The uncomfortable, awkward, tough-to-spit-out truth. The thing you've been holding back because you're afraid of ruffling feathers, offending someone, or making things weird. Let me put this bluntly—holding back helps no one. In fact, it's where most communication breaks down. You *think* you're sparing someone's feelings, or avoiding conflict, but in reality, you're building walls, creating distance, and breeding resentment.

Stop hiding behind the fear of fallout. You're not doing anyone any favors by holding back. Not at work, not with your partner, not in any relationship. If something's on your mind, **say it.** You have to give people the opportunity to hear and respond to what you're thinking. Yes, it's risky. Yes, it's uncomfortable. But you know what's even worse? Watching something fall apart because you were too scared to speak up.

Remember your why? The one you've been carrying with you since chapter one? That why can be solved when you step up and say the damn thing. Your life will never change if you keep skirting around the tough stuff. You won't grow, your relationships won't thrive, and your career won't progress. If you can't speak the truth in a moment that matters, what are you even doing? By asking the question and saying the thing, you're laying the groundwork for better communication, stronger relationships, and—wait for it—a life that's more in line with who you really are. And isn't that what this is all about? Taking control of the way you interact with the world and making it work for you?

Look, I'm not trying to sprinkle glitter on a pile of crap here. I know this isn't easy. But if you want real change, if you want to lead with Kind Transparency, then you've gotta ask, and you've gotta say. Anything less is just a waste of everyone's time.

6

People don't change

I'm probably going to get some opposition to this, but I want to openly talk about something that is said far too often.

People don't change

I'm here to definitively say that I am not interested in hearing that tired, lazy-a$$ excuse anymore. "People don't change," you say? That's just something we've been conditioned to believe when things get hard or uncomfortable. It's the ultimate cop-out. It's a convenient way to say, "I'm done trying," without admitting that you've thrown in the towel. Sure, people have their habits, their deeply ingrained reactions, their autopilot responses—but to say they are stuck forever? Please. That's like saying, "Birds can't fly," just because you've been watching a penguin struggle across the ice. Don't confuse one bad example with the whole picture.

Remember conditioning? It's the stuff that sets up the initial programming in your brain; your triggers and responses. Those programs are not made out of stone, it's more like a bunch of LEGO blocks. Sure, it's sturdy, but with a little self-awareness and some elbow grease, you can yank those pieces apart and reconfigure them into something that actually serves who you are today. It's going to be messy, and yeah, you might step on a few metaphorical LEGO pieces along the way (ouch), but that's part of the process. The point is, you have the power to remodel and build something that fits who you want to be, not just who you've been told you are.

Now let's talk about trauma. I mean openly talk about it. Like we've already discussed, many people use it as an excuse or a crutch to justify certain behaviors. But let's be real here: trauma is not your life's story. It's a chapter – maybe a brutal, gut-wrenching one – but it's not the whole damn book. You get to decide how the next chapters are written. With the right support, a hell of a lot of work, and a willingness to confront the ugly parts of your past, you can take that story and steer it in a different direction. Does it mean erasing the pain? Absolutely not. But it does not mean letting that pain control you.

And listen, I'm not just sitting here preaching some "rah-rah, you can do it" motivational BS. These are facts: Change is not only possible; it's essential. If you're not changing, you're stagnating, and that's the fastest way to kill off any potential for growth, connection, or happiness in your life. So, stop hiding behind the excuse that you're "just wired this way" or that "people can't change." That's a cop-out, and you know it. Growth is uncomfortable. It's awkward. But it's a hell of a lot better than being stuck in a version of yourself that no longer serves you.

Let's clear something else up about change, though, because this is where people get it twisted. When I say people can change, I'm not talking about some Hollywood-level personality overhaul. There are parts of who you are (like your temperaments, your core traits) that are going to be with you forever. That's just biology, own it. But here are the levers: You can change how you react to those traits, those triggers, those knee-jerk responses that used to send you spiraling.

People absolutely have the ability to change their habits and conditioning. The question is, and this is the real question, how badly do you want it? Are you motivated enough to do the hard, uncomfortable work of confronting yourself? And let's not forget about your environment. Because if you're trying to change while surrounded by people who keep dragging you back into the same old patterns, you're setting yourself up for failure.

So, here's a very simple truth: Change is all about two key things – 'motivation' and 'environment'.

- Are you in a space that's going to help you evolve, or are you clinging to a toxic setting because it's comfortable?
- Are you ready to confront your own BS, or are you going to keep pretending that it's everyone else's problem?

People can change. You can change. But it's not going to happen by wishing on a star or waiting for the universe to hand you an epiphany. You've got to be willing to tear down the parts of yourself that aren't working and rebuild something better, brick by damn brick.

Speaking further of change, the problem isn't really change itself, it's the idea of control. Here's where most people go off the rails. When they talk about change, what they *really* mean is control. And let's be real for a second—you can't control people. No matter how hard you try, you can't make someone do something they don't want to do. The only thing you can control? **You**. Your actions, your reactions, and your attitude. But people don't like hearing that. Control is like a security blanket. It gives us a false sense of comfort, makes us believe we can bend the world (or others) to our will. And when we realize we can't? That's when the resentment, the frustration, and the rage come pouring in.

> Control and influence are two very different things.

If you can't understand that, you're going to constantly set yourself up for disappointment. Control means making all the decisions, having total power over something or someone. Influence? That's how you affect the decisions and actions of others *without* taking away their agency.

Let's look at some examples:

> You've driven a car, right? You control the wheel, the speed, and how safely you drive. But can you control the idiot in the next lane who's texting while speeding down the highway? Nope. You can't control him, but you can influence the situation by turning on your turn signal, slowing down, or giving him some extra space. You're impacting the outcome of the situation without taking over the his control.

> Or imagine this: You're paddling a boat down a river. You can't control the current. Once you're in the water, that's the way you're going. But, you can influence where you go by grabbing a paddle and starting to steer.

Get it? When you confuse **influence** with **control**, you're setting yourself up for failure. And not just that—you're setting fire to your relationships, your peace of mind, and probably your own damn happiness. You'll be disappointed when people don't do what you expect. But (spoiler alert) they don't have to.

Now, let's talk about what happens when these concepts intersect. Picture two circles. One is your Sphere of Control. This is where you reign supreme. You call the shots, make the decisions, and control what happens. This is your behavior, your actions, your choices. Then, there's the Sphere of Influence. This is where your behavior has an effect on the people around you, on situations that you can't directly control but can *influence*. The bigger your sphere of influence, the more you can inspire, impact, and change outcomes. Outside of these two spheres? That's the Sphere of Concern. This is where most people waste their energy. It's all the nonsense that keeps you up at night: the weather, other people's opinions, global crises, the guy who didn't text you back. But guess what? You can't control it. You can't even influence most of it. So why the hell are you wasting your time stressing about it?

Focus your energy where it matters—on what you can control and what you can influence. Everything else? Let it go. Because that sh*t is just noise. Let's talk about relationships, the one-to-one, face-to-face, no-hiding-behind-excuses kind of relationships. This is where influence and control get really murky, and it's where most people screw up big time.

Imagine two people, each with their own Sphere of Control and Sphere of Influence. They overlap like a Venn diagram. The part where they overlap? That's where collaboration, respect, and healthy influence happen. Both people have influence over one another (sometimes small, sometimes big) but they each still maintain control over their own decisions, behaviors, and external influences.

But, here's where the balance gets tricky. Let's say Person 1 starts pushing their influence too far. Their sphere starts creeping into Person 2's space, taking up more and more room. Maybe they start telling them what to do, how to think, how to act. Maybe they make decisions for them without asking. Person 2's sphere shrinks. Soon, they're not just influenced by Person 1, they're being controlled by them. They lose their ability to make choices about external things because they've been consumed by the over-influence of Person 1.

That's not influence anymore. That's control, and it's <u>toxic as hell</u>.

When this happens, the relationship becomes a power struggle, even if one person doesn't realize it. Person 2 starts feeling suffocated, angry, and powerless. Person 1, on the other hand, might feel empowered, like they've "fixed" things or are "helping." But really, they've bulldozed right over the boundaries of healthy influence and into the toxic territory of control. There is a very thin line here, and it's so easy to let it slip. It happens slowly, over time and is difficult to walk back from.

In any healthy relationship (personal, professional, whatever) there needs to be **mutual influence**. You have to let the other person have their space, their control, their ability to affect change in the world around them. Sure, you can influence each other, but once you start infringing on their right to make decisions, you're not building a connection—you're building a dictatorship.

So, where's the line?

It's simple: Influence is about impact, not control. You can guide, suggest, and inspire. You can lead by example. But the minute you start dictating how someone else should act or think, or feel, you've crossed the line. You've taken away their control. Want to know why your relationships feel strained? Why people push back when you try to "help"? It's because they feel like you're trying to control them instead of influence them. No one wants to be told what to do, they want to be guided toward making the right decision for *themselves.*

Control might feel good in the short term, but in the long run? It destroys trust, breeds resentment, and kills relationships faster than you can say "my way or the highway." So ask yourself: are you influencing, or are you controlling? And if you've been trying to control someone, take a step back and reevaluate. Give them their space back. Let them have their own Sphere of Control, and focus on what you can influence without overstepping your bounds. And most importantly? Stop wasting everyones energy worrying about sh*t you can't control or influence. We all deserve better than that.

Story Time

I'd like to take you down a bit of a rabbit hole for this one, if you'll follow me? A short background first, then we'll bring it full circle! In the mid-20th century, there was a psychological researcher named Bruce Tuckman. The primary focus of his research was centered around group dynamics. In 1965, he published a theory known as "Tuckman's stages of group development". Now, Tuckman's work is typically used in reference to organizational or extracurricular team management. However, I would like to take a slightly different perspective and apply these concepts to any human relationship.

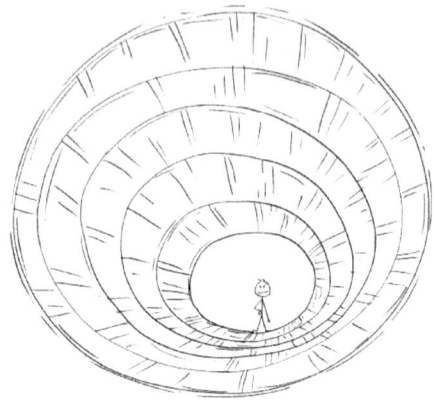

Tuckman's stages of group development is a well-known framework that describes the various phases a team typically goes through in its journey toward becoming a highly functioning unit. In the context of what we have been discussing, these stages can provide valuable insights into how the introduction or removal of variables can impact relationships. Let's explore each stage and how they relate to the various challenges we encounter with difficult people:

Forming - "Getting to Know You"

Consider this the beginning of any relationship or team dynamic. You meet someone new; you start a new job; you get added to a new project... etc. In the Forming stage, people are polite and cautiously getting to know one another. This is where we lay the foundation for the dynamics of the relationship. Encouraging open but respectful communication at this point sets a precedent. People should feel safe expressing themselves honestly while considering the feelings and perspectives of others. Typically, people are on their best behavior during this stage.

Storming - "Navigating Conflicts"

The Storming phase is where people's true nature starts to emerge. As people start to work together, conflicts and differences in opinions may emerge. People get more comfortable and drop any sense of pretense that previously existed. This stage is a pivotal milestone that will determine the trajectory for the remainder of the engagement. In an ideal world, people would openly address conflicts with kindness and empathy. This would be an opportunity for people to practice active listening and attempt to understand each other's viewpoints. However, we know that this is not what happens in reality.

Norming - "Establishing Cohesion"

If a group of people can rise beyond the Storming phase and begin to find common ground, they move into the Norming phase. This is where we settle into our roles and establish norms for interaction. People have defined their boundaries and set expectations. This is a good time within a team or relationship, but they can't get too comfortable. It is very easy to get pulled back down into Storming. They must continue to ensure that all voices are heard, and that they strive to reach consensus on the important things.

Performing - "Effective Collaboration"

Once a group effectively masters the Norming phase, they can start Performing. When people no longer spend their time and energy arguing and complaining, they can focus that energy on improving. In this phase, people are highly productive and efficient. They use the common ground they've developed to collaborate on shared goals. But, just as before, consistency continues to be a guiding principle, reinforcing the idea that successful collaboration is built on honesty and trust. People can freely share ideas, feedback, and concerns with the confidence that they will be treated with kindness and respect.

Adjourning - "Closure and Reflection"

While Tuckman's model didn't originally include this stage, it's a critical part of any groups journey. Many relationships end for one reason or another, but in this phase, we are discussing the ones that disband or transition on good terms. People might move, change jobs, start new projects, or any number of other life-changing situations. It's important in these times to take a reflective approach. People should openly discuss the accomplishments and challenges, acknowledging both successes and areas for improvement. It's an opportunity to part ways with gratitude and positive feedback.

In the context of Kind Transparency, Tuckman's model becomes a roadmap for people to navigate their development stages with compassion, understanding, and openness. It reinforces the idea that transparent and empathetic communication is a vital component that touches every phase of group dynamics, ultimately leading to more successful and harmonious collaborations.

So, great. That is a thing you know now. How is it going to help you deal with difficult people in difficult situations? Well, I challenge you to add this theory as a tool in your toolbelt when approaching conversations. For each relationship dynamic you have, define what phase you are in. Then, determine what would need to be true for you to move on to the next phase.

Think about your team at work, your boss, your friend group, or your significant other. Did you just meet? Are you in constant confrontation? Is it just sort of a status quo? Or are you super effective together? Understanding where you are at, and why, is incredibly valuable in being able to affect change.

Now, to throw in another layer of complexity, even the best of relationships ebb and flow throughout these phases. You can work and grow and finally reach the Performing stage, but at any point, an external variable can come crashing in like the Kool-Aid man and send you spiraling your way back to Forming. What do I mean by this? Here are some very common examples:

- A new team member gets hired and joins an existing team. Everyone goes back to Forming, because they must now bring this person into their group dynamic. Time is taken away from performing to bring this person up to speed, train them, explain boundaries and expectations.
- A couple gets pregnant and has a child. The child forms a new group dynamic, forcing them to relearn who they are in relation to this new family unit and what that means for each of them. New roles, responsibilities and boundaries are introduced that need to be redefined.
- Someone gets injured or has a traumatic life event and can no longer go out and participate in activities with their friends like

they once did. The group of friends would move back to Storming, because their norm has been disrupted. They will need to determine if they alter their activities to accommodate their friends' situation or move on without them.

In any case, the ultimate testament to a person or groups' resilience is how quickly they can move back to Performing after an external variable has knocked them down. When you approach a conversation through the lens of this dynamic, you can determine how and where you need to focus. And conversely, if someone has changed, or you've suddenly felt a shift in the dynamic of your relationship, but you don't know why, this is a shiny beacon telling you that something needs fixed.

So, when it is said that people don't change, I point back to this theory. It can be extrapolated to represent a single person as they transact throughout their life. People can and do change, but it's in relation to context and triggers. A person can be a high functioning and consistent for years, until a life altering event occurs. This trigger can elicit a negative behavioral response that they always had a predisposition towards, but never came out until this situation. Conversely, someone who lives in a constant state of trigger will continue to portray certain negative behavioral responses until they are able to move out of that cycle back into the Norming and Performing phases.

External variables, triggers and change are the catalysts that send us through a roller coaster of developmental phases. We all ebb and flow through the ups and downs of life. The more fluid that motion, and the quicker we can progress through the stages, the sooner we can get back to a place of stability.

Alright, so if you've made it this far, and if you're still telling yourself that people don't change, you've either not paying attention or you're just plain stubborn. So, let me try one last dose of reality. Successful relationships, just like people, are not static. They're not some perfectly crafted garden where everything blooms just right after one good rainfall. Relationships are messy, unpredictable, and often a total pain in the a$$—just like real life. And you know what? That's exactly why they're worth the effort.

There's this myth out there that you can just "set it and forget it" when it comes to human connections. If you haven't picked it up yet, (spoiler alert) that's not how this works. That's not how *any* of this works. Relationships—whether they're personal, professional, or somewhere in between—demand constant effort, intentionally, and the willingness to get your hands dirty. They demand you to be present, to actively engage, and to be brutally honest with yourself about who you are and who you want to be.

Here's where the whole "people don't change" nonsense falls apart: If you're in a relationship, you are either evolving, or you're rotting. It's that simple. And this isn't just about the other person; it's about *you*. You've got to put in the work to adapt, grow, and yes—change. Because if you're not willing to evolve, to meet people where they are, and to have those tough conversations when it's uncomfortable, then you're not just stalling; you're actively killing the potential of that relationship.

Think about it: Every time you choose to dismiss the possibility of change, you're taking the easy way out. You're saying, "I don't have the energy to make this better," or "I'm not willing to step outside my comfort zone." And if that's the attitude you want to take, fine—just don't expect anything meaningful to come out of it. Real change requires you to dig deep, confront your own bullshit, and have the courage to do the same for others.

You don't get to say, "Oh, that's just the way I am," and expect everyone to just deal with it. That's a lazy cop-out, and it's a slap in the face to the people who *are* willing to put in the work. It's also disrespectful to yourself because you're telling yourself that you're not capable of more, of better, of *evolving*.

You deserve better.

Remember Tuckman's stages? That's your roadmap, not just for group dynamics but for life. It's proof that change isn't just possible; it's *inevitable*, and cyclical. Whether you like it or not, you're going to go through those phases over and over again. So why not be intentional about it? Why not embrace the storming, the norming, and the performing phases as opportunities to grow, instead of dreading them?

When you truly understand and accept that people are always in a state of flux—moving in and out of these stages—you stop seeing them as "fixed" beings and start seeing them for what they really are: *works in progress*. And that, my friend, is where the People Magic happens. That's where you get to witness real transformation, where you get to play a part in helping someone move from storming to performing. That's where you build the kind of connections that actually mean something.

And yes, it's going to be messy. It's going to be uncomfortable. There will be times when you'll question whether it's worth the effort. (*It absolutely is.*) Because every time you lean in, every time you choose to give a damn, every time you decide that you're not going to settle for surface-level interactions—you're proving that people can change. You're proving that growth isn't just a possibility; it's a reality.

So, the next time someone tells you that "people don't change," smile, nod, and keep moving forward. Because you'll know the truth. You'll know that change is not only possible—it's happening all around you, all the time. And you get to be a part of it. You get to be the catalyst, the guide, the one who sees beyond the bullshit and calls out the potential for greatness in others.

That's what Kind Transparency is all about. It's not about pretending that change is easy. It's about acknowledging that it's hard as hell, but worth every ounce of effort. So stop hiding, stop making excuses, and start doing the work. Because people *do* change—when they have the courage, the support, and the environment that allows them to do so.

You've got the tools. You've got the knowledge. Now, go out there and make it happen.

7

Sometimes people are a$$holes

I wish it weren't true, but it is. It would be silly and negligent to try to write a book about communication and connection without addressing the elephant in the room. You are going to run into people who are not pleasant and seemingly unwilling to budge no matter how hard you try.

Not every difficult person you meet is a narcissist, but they do exist. However, more often than not, as we just discussed, people have baggage and trauma that they cannot or are not willing to fix. Now you're asking - How do I react to an immovable problem?

Don't.

When a person is adamant about something and they are willing to die on their hill, regardless of the truth, perception or social contracts at play, they are looking for resistance. So, don't react. Don't give them the benefit of knowing the sentiment of your opposition, because that will put them in a position of power.

Gaining and maintaining power during a conversation can be a critical skill. When you're confronted with someone who is unyielding in their stance, willing to defend their position with unwavering determination, you're essentially navigating a battlefield of ideas. This person is looking for a point of contention to assert their authority and dominance. It's a power play that requires a strategic response.

The key to handling these situations is not to react impulsively. By resisting the urge to react emotionally or with immediate opposition, you can avoid falling into their carefully laid traps. Providing them with a glimpse into your state of mind too soon hands them the upper hand, granting them control over the conversation.

To seize and retain power in such encounters, you should adopt a mindful approach. Start by actively listening to their perspective. This sends a powerful message: you value their viewpoint, even if it differs from your own. Allow them to express their thoughts, giving them the space to elaborate on their stance. This approach subtly shifts the balance of power, as they no longer perceive you as a direct threat or a source of resistance.

As the conversation progresses, you can then carefully introduce your own viewpoint. Present your argument logically, relying on facts and reasoning, rather than emotions. By doing so, you establish yourself as a formidable, level-headed participant in the discussion.

Moreover, emphasizing common ground can be a potent tactic. Identifying areas of agreement, no matter how small, can lead to a shift in power dynamics. As the conversation evolves, focus on building bridges and finding shared interests. This collaborative spirit can help dissolve the adversarial atmosphere and pave the way for a more constructive dialogue.

Think of yourself as a double agent, sent to infiltrate an enemy compound. You blend in, adapt your conversation style so as not to draw attention to yourself, coaxing out more and more information until you have what you need. Inevitably, they will reveal the kink in their armor. The unlocked gate that will allow you to advance your ideas and thoughts, slowly weakening their defenses.

In essence, the art of gaining and maintaining power during challenging conversations is about restraint, strategy, and patience. Don't provide your opposition with the immediate satisfaction of resistance. Instead, approach the conversation as a collaborative endeavor, creating a space for productive discourse. In doing so, you'll find yourself in a stronger position to influence the dialogue and navigate even the most arduous discussions.

These people; let's call them the villains of their own story. They are incapable of seeing things from any perspective but their own.

- **The Gaston:** Overflowing with confidence and arrogance, they're masters at bending narratives to suit their preferences.
- **The Eric Cartman:** They seem to relish chaos, often engaging in offensive behavior purely for the attention it garners.
- **The Squidward:** A never-ending search for faults and flaws, even in life's most flawless moments.
- **(He Who Shall Not Be Named):** Carrying grudges like badges of honor, they seem unable to release the past's perceived wrongs.
- **The Evil Queen:** Driven by jealousy, vanity, and an unyielding commitment to their own desires.

No matter how hard you try, or what jedi mind tricks you use, there will be people and situations that could be too far gone. That's ok, it's even good in some sense because you know where you stand

and how to react. In these instances, it's essential to recognize that this is a normal part of the human experience. It's a bit like searching for a signal in a remote area with a failing GPS – no matter how advanced the technology, there are areas it can't reach.

Now, here's the silver lining in these seemingly challenging situations: sometimes, they are a blessing in disguise. They serve as a litmus test, making it clear where we stand and how to react. When we confront the unyielding, we gain clarity about our boundaries, values, and priorities. These situations push us to define what is non-negotiable in our lives.

However, there's an intriguing twist – when you do step back, creating space and accepting that not everything is within your control, sometimes, just sometimes, those very individuals or scenarios that initially seemed out of reach can surprise you. As you disengage from the battle, they may find it within themselves to step forward and bridge the gap. This is a testament to the profound power of vulnerability and resilience inherent in all of us. It's a reminder that true connection often happens when we least expect it, and it's something we can all nurture.

But you've been through a lot. Why should you care? You feel like no one else cares, so what's the point? Because - nothing changes if you do nothing.

Ok, so the big question really is; what do you do when you have no choice but to deal with a difficult person in a difficult situation? First, we need to square with the fact that if we're in the situation, we might as well make the best of it. It takes just as much effort to complain and fight against something as it does to just get through it and do what you can to make the best of the situation.

> "If you can't get out of it, get into it!"
> Quaritch (Avatar 2)

Embrace the possibility of a losing outcome.

When it comes to practicing Kind Transparency, one essential aspect is preparing yourself for the possibility of a losing outcome. But what does that mean, and why is it important? In the realm of human interactions, a "losing outcome" doesn't necessarily imply a competition or battle. Instead, it refers to situations where your expectations may not be met, where your best efforts at transparent and compassionate communication may not yield the results you hoped for.

Why is it crucial to embrace this idea? First and foremost, because life is unpredictable. No matter how skilled you become at communicating kindly and transparently, there will always be factors beyond your control. Others may not respond as you anticipated, and circumstances may take unexpected turns. Here's where the concept of emotional resilience comes into play. Preparing for a potential "losing outcome" means recognizing that not every interaction will go as planned. It means understanding that despite your best intentions, you may encounter resistance, misunderstanding, or even rejection.

However, this should not deter you from practicing Kind Transparency. In fact, it's a fundamental part of the learning process. Here are a few reasons why embracing the possibility of a losing outcome is so important:

1. **Realistic Expectations:** Acknowledging the potential for less-than-ideal outcomes keeps your expectations grounded in reality. You recognize that while you can control your

communication and approach, you can't control how others will respond.
2. **Growth Through Challenges:** Just like any skill, practicing Kind Transparency is a journey filled with challenges and learning experiences. When you encounter a "losing outcome," it's an opportunity for growth and self-improvement. It's a chance to reflect on what could have been done differently and to adapt your approach.
3. **Strengthening Resilience:** Dealing with situations that don't go as planned builds emotional resilience. It teaches you to handle disappointment, frustration, and setbacks without losing sight of your commitment to kindness and transparency.
4. **Authenticity in Communication:** The willingness to accept losing outcomes can paradoxically lead to more authentic and transparent communication. When people sense that you're genuine and not just focused on winning, they are often more open to honest and constructive dialogue.
5. **Fostering Trust:** Knowing that you can accept less favorable results can increase your credibility and trustworthiness in the eyes of others. People appreciate honesty and vulnerability, even in challenging moments.

In essence, preparing for a losing outcome is about approaching Kind Transparency with a realistic and open-hearted mindset. It's about focusing on the process of communication, rather than fixating on specific outcomes. When you do this, every interaction, even those that don't go as planned, becomes an opportunity for growth, connection, and self-improvement.

Story Time

I once was managing a project team who was tasked with building a very complex enterprise application that would be used by thousands of people. This team had their work cut out for them! Not only did they have a limited timeline and budget, but they also had to merge in an external vendor team that the customer was already working with!

Needless to say, the team dynamic devolved back into "forming" (more on this later). There were 2 personalities on this newly formed team which were in stark contrast. It just happened to be the team leads from each respective team. We will call them James and Marcus. They disagreed about everything, and openly argued in group settings.

It was disruptive, and impacted every aspect of the project. Something had to be done, so following the rules of Kind Transparency:

I first had breakout sessions with each person in an effort to get to know them better. Background, work history, family, hobbies...etc. I asked some leading questions like: "What role did you play in that project?", "How do you feel about the outcome?", "What outlets do you have to express yourself and be creative?"

And look, this is management 101 type stuff. That isn't what we are talking about here, you can read that in every management book in the last 3 decades. What is different, and what I need you to hear, is that I came to the conversation from a place of vulnerability. I let them know that I had skin in the game. The outcome of this project and their success was my responsibility. I then expressed my concerns, and where I was struggling.

I am a pretty technical person, and understood most of what they were doing, but I am not a Technical Architect. So, instead of making assumptions, or simply asking them what they do, I asked them to "teach" me. (Even if you know something, hearing it from another person's perspective can be very valuable in understanding where they are at.) Most people take great pride in what they do, and when given the right opportunity love to speak about it. So, I listened intently as they described what they were building and how. I took detailed notes on architecture, design, optimization and anything else they were willing to tell me.

I did this with each person on the team, and what I learned was fascinating. Each person cared SO much. These were consummate professionals who were all marching towards a very big goal. The problem was that they were either marching in different directions or stepping on each other's feet. This was a breakthrough.

The root of the discourse ended up being a differing opinion in the design of the structural code. Think of it like the foundation of a house. We had an immediate need to build a 2 bedroom, 1 bathroom house. People needed to move in soon! But, we knew that soon after we would need to expand that house to accommodate 2 more bedrooms and one additional bathroom.

One person wanted to build out a solid foundation that would support all 4 bedrooms and 2 baths now, while the other person wanted to build only what we needed now, and build the whole addition later. Neither person was wrong, and neither was right. Sometimes there is not a 'right' answer, just a more right answer given a collection of circumstances. That is where we were.

So, I decided to take the decision away from them. Because sometimes, when people have such strong opinions and have laid such solid claims, it is very hard to back down from those positions. I gave them an out. We went to the business team and division manager with all of the facts and asked them to give priority to one solution over the other. Ultimately, we ended on a bit of a compromise that allowed for speed in certain areas but a more robust build out of others. The reason we were able to get there is that we removed the point of contention. Everyone felt heard, and even if they didn't get exactly what they wanted, they had a seat at the table, which is typically what matters. This allowed everyone to step down off their high towers and put away their pitchforks.

However, this isn't a cure, it requires continued work and maintenance. As we know, people can easily slip back into habits. But eventually, it got to a point where all I needed to do was send a DM during a conference call that said, "Do you need a Snickers?", and they would understand that they were being grumpy and going a bit too far, and would reel themselves in. We would then have an open conversation about their concerns after.

Don't let me fool you; this doesn't happen over one conversation or a single intervention. This allegory has a bit of movie magic.

This is an actual note I sent to one of my teams after a particularly tense week:

"*Hey @channel! I've been thinking about you guys a lot the last couple of days and just wanted to drop this here.*

Obviously, it's my job to keep the clients happy, but more than that, it's my duty to make sure all of you are happy. You are all my most important customers, and it hurts my soul when you guys are struggling. Reading through the chat history in both channels there are a few things that are apparent to me as an outside observer, and I thought it might be helpful for you to hear them.

First, you all are amazing at what you do. This couldn't be more evident. When we first started this project, we were very hesitant and had a huge mountain to climb to get past [client 1] and [client 2]'s comfort zone, and [client 3]'s reluctance to spend money. But you did it. You proved yourself, you built that trust, and you've continued to provide them with value.

Secondly, you all are incredibly passionate about what you do. You care SO MUCH about the project and the success of what you are doing. This passion is why there are disagreements. If no one cared, you guys would be no better than [competitor], shoving square pegs into round holes just to say you did something. So, while this can be frustrating, I've been doing this a long time, and this is the ultimate catalyst to a high functioning team.

Lastly, we have to remember that people experience the world through their own paradigms, and people intrinsically act from their own motivations. You are all saying the same thing and are marching toward the same goals. Sometimes it's hard to see that when you're so close to it, and it's easy to get caught up in pride and ego. Often, there isn't a right answer, there is just an answer for the moment, given everything we know, and it's ok to disagree. It's even ok to be wrong; we move forward.

We are all in this together. Please don't feel like the weight of the project or any one decision lays solely on your shoulders. Leverage your team. If you get stuck, reach out. When we have differing opinions, let's stop, reset, and do a quick cost/benefit analysis. And ultimately, it's up to the client to decide which direction we go in, good – bad – or ugly. We are just here to advise and be the best stewards of our craft that we can be."

Taking Action

You're not a superhero, and you're not expected to have all the answers right away. Let's be honest, the pressure to always respond immediately in tough situations is one of the biggest reasons people end up saying something they regret. Newsflash: You are **never obligated** to react on the spot. (Say it louder for the people in the back!) If anything, the expectation that you should have an answer at the drop of a hat is absurd. So, here's your permission slip to take a step back, breathe, and **reset**.

> "Poor planning on your part does not constitute an emergency on my part"
> Bob Carter

Sometimes, taking no action immediately is the most powerful action you can take. Why? Because you're giving yourself the opportunity to really think it through, to respond with intention instead of reacting out of panic, anger, or ego. It's okay to admit that you need time. Hell, it's more than okay—it's smart. Here's one way to approach it:

"This new information is important to my understanding of the situation. I'd like to take a bit of time to process this and come back to you by the end of the day with a more thoughtful response."

Notice what that does? It puts you back in control of the conversation. You're not letting the other person's urgency dictate your response. You're not throwing words into the air just to fill the silence. You're being **intentional**.

Now that you've slowed down and given yourself some time, let's get into the strategy. There's a process here, and I'm going to break it down step-by-step.

Mirror

Mirroring is NOT just parroting back someone's words. (Even though it fun to mock your siblings in that way.) What I'm talking about here is reflecting the emotion, energy, or tone that the other person is giving you. It's not manipulation; it's validation. You're essentially saying, "I see you; I hear you, and we're on the same wavelength."

> *"I can see that you're frustrated, and I understand that this situation feels unfair to you."*

When you mirror someone, you're showing empathy without necessarily agreeing, which is the key differentiator. You're acknowledging their experience without validating their opinion or behavior, which opens the door for further conversation. And trust me, nothing disarms a person faster than feeling genuinely understood.

Label

Labeling is basically calling out the elephant in the room. You put a name to what's happening, what's being felt, or what's really at stake. It's honest, it's direct, and it's the fastest way to cut through the bullshit.

"It sounds like you're feeling unappreciated and overlooked in this project."

Why label? Because the minute you put a name to it, you take away some of its power. Consider "He who must not be named", by avoiding saying his name the people of the wizarding world give him an almost mythical level of fear and power. But, when Harry and the others start using his real name, it signified that they were no longer afraid, and it released the control he had over them.

Define boundaries

Here's where the magic happens. You set the terms of engagement. You're not just letting the other person know what you won't tolerate—you're defining what's acceptable moving forward.

Example:

"I understand how you feel, but this behavior isn't acceptable if we're going to work together effectively. Moving forward, here's what I need from you..."

Or:

"The bottom line is this: I respect your perspective, but this is how we're going to proceed. If that's a deal-breaker, let's figure out what happens next."

Boundaries aren't walls; they're guidelines. They tell people how they can engage with you. And guess what? Most people will respect those boundaries once you're clear about them. The ones who don't? They're the ones who need the hardest boundaries of all.

Walk away

I am always the first person to tell you to try, and care, and be consistent. Time and persistence typically win. But, if you've mirrored, labeled, and defined your boundaries, and the other person still isn't getting it? It's time to walk away. And I mean that—literally or figuratively. At some point, you have to realize that you've done everything you can. Continuing to engage is just wasting your time, energy and sanity.

Example:

"I hear you, and I've heard you. But if you can't trust/adopt/accept this position, there isn't much more I can say. I'll let actions speak louder than words."

Let that sink in. You're not abandoning the conversation; you're acknowledging that it's reached its limit in its current state. You've said your piece, you've laid out your expectations, and now it's up to them to meet you halfway. If they can't add collateral to the exchange, the deal is off.

Sometimes you have to rip the Band-Aid off

Here's the part nobody wants to talk about: Sometimes, you've got to face the music and tear that band-aid off. It's not going to be pretty, it's not going to feel good, but it's necessary. Maybe you've been tiptoeing around an issue for far too long, or maybe you've been waiting for the "right" moment to address something that's been festering. Newsflash: There is no right moment.

The longer you avoid it, the worse it's going to get. So, when you know you need to act, just do it. Yes, it's going to be uncomfortable. Yes, it might ruffle some feathers. But delaying that discomfort only compounds the problem. Address it head-on, own your truth, and move forward.

At the end of the day, taking action isn't about controlling the outcome; it's about taking control of how you show up. It's about being clear, intentional, and unapologetically yourself—even when it's hard. And trust me, that's where the real growth happens.

So, stop waiting for permission, stop hesitating, and start taking action. It's not always going to be easy, but damn, it's going to be **worth it.**

8

Embrace the chaos

As we've already discussed, life doesn't come with an instruction manual, a pause button, or a magic escape hatch. Sometimes, you're handed a situation that feels like a dumpster fire wrapped in barbed wire. You can't always control the environment, the people you're surrounded by, or the circumstances that come barreling into your life like a runaway freight train. However, you do have control over how you react, adapt, and respond.

"Embrace the chaos" isn't just a cute little catchphrase – it's a survival strategy. It's taking a look at the mess in front of you and thinking, "Alright, this is where we're at. Now what?" You have a choice, a fork in the road. You can suffer through, complain endlessly, or worse, let the situation consume you, or you can lean in, flip the script, and turn it into an opportunity, a learning experience, or even a great lesson learned for your next blog post.

There are going to be moments where you're stuck – no exit, no turning back, no quick fix. It's that family reunion where Aunt Karen keeps asking about your personal life, the project you're assigned at work with the coworker who thinks deadlines are a suggestion, or that school group project where you somehow end up doing all the work.

The reality is - you can't always walk away. You have to acknowledge that some situations are inevitable. But contrary to popular belief, wallowing in self-misery doesn't solve anything. Remember quicksand? The more you struggle against it, the deeper you sink. (They really had us thinking quicksand was going to be a big problem in our lives, didn't they?)

The first step? Accept that you're here and stop wasting energy wishing that you weren't.

Example Situations:

- The family event you can't avoid but desperately want to. (*Searches how to fake your own death.*)
- The unplanned work emergency that conveniently arrives at the worst possible moment.
- Your kids school calls because they are sick, right before a really important appointment.

Alright, so you've accepted that you're in this mess. Now what? Here's where most people either start spiraling or get stuck in a "pity cycle". Not you. <u>Not today</u>. Instead, you're going to wake up and choose **stability**. You're going to control the things you can control, and work around the things that you cannot. And you're going to do it with a mindset shift.

Complaining won't make things better – it just spreads negativity like glitter at a preschool birthday party. It's sticky, gets everywhere, and is impossible to clean up. Instead, ask yourself: How can I take this situation and turn it into something worth my time and energy? This is where you stop playing the victim and start playing the game.

You're the architect of your own chaos.

If I'm being honest, sometimes we're our own worst enemies. We forget important documents, over-commit ourselves, or procrastinate until the VERY last minute. It's easy to get caught up in frustration and blame everything and everyone around you. But the real growth comes when you own up to your part in the chaos and decide to fix it.

As a mother, a wife, a project manager, and people leader, I run into seemingly impossible situations all the time. Here are a few off the top of my head:

- Forms and money that are due and forgotten at home
- School projects due tomorrow that we don't have the supplies for
- Unplanned projects or trips that completely rework our schedule
- Scope creep, budget restrictions or timeline changes
- Someone at work quit and you we're already short staffed
- You get in a car accident that is maybe at least partially your fault
- Someone close to you gets sick and won't listen to Dr's orders

What's the point in crying over spilled milk when you could just go get a milkshake instead? Sure, the situation sucks. But instead of being mad at the universe, grab a towel, clean it up, and then treat yourself to something better. When you own up to your role in the mess, it becomes easier to shift gears, problem-solve, and make the most of what you have to work with.

There's no rule that says you have to be miserable just because the situation is. Humor, curiosity, and a willingness to be flexible will take you far in life. Let's be clear: laughing in the face of adversity isn't about ignoring the problem – it's about taking away its power to ruin your day.

Forget to turn in an important document by it's due date? Instead of panicking, turn it into a game. How fast can you get it done? How creative can you be with your excuses? Is it ridiculous? Absolutely. But it takes the edge off, and allows you to handle it more calmly and efficiently. If you can't get out of it, get into it! Make it an adventure, something worth talking about later. Spin the narrative so you're not just a passive participant – you're the main character in this dumpster fire of a narrative.

> "Don't Let a Ruined Moment Ruin Your Whole Day"
> My Husband

This might be the single greatest piece of advice I've ever received, and I'm not just saying that because I'm married to him. It's a brilliant reminder that bad moments are inevitable, but letting them snowball into bad hours, bad days, or bad weeks is entirely optional. You get to decide how much power a single moment has over your entire day.

Think about it: you're running late to a meeting, you spill coffee on your shirt, and now you're mad at the world. But does that mean you need to carry that frustration with you to every single interaction for the rest of the day? Absolutely not. Wipe off the coffee, laugh at yourself, and move on.

I'll listen to your complaints once, but after that, I want solutions.

Venting is necessary sometimes. I get it. We all need a moment to scream into the void. But once you've let it out, it's time to pivot. Don't come to me with the same problem twice unless you're ready to talk about potential solutions. Yes, life is hard. Yes, people are difficult. But complaining without action is like sitting in a sinking boat and refusing to pick up a bucket. If you're not actively trying to bail yourself out, then you're just watching the water rise.

"You're right, it's not my circus, not my monkeys" – said no leader ever. Because guess what? It *is* your circus, and those *are* your monkeys, especially if you're a parent, a manager, a friend, or a partner. You signed up for this, remember? So, embrace the role, grab a megaphone, and start figuring out how to make this circus the best damn show in town. When you stop fighting against the reality of your responsibilities and start taking ownership, you realize just how much influence you actually have over the situation. Instead of being the person who says, "Not my problem," be the person who says, "How can we fix this?"

The ultimate skill in embracing chaos is learning how to see every challenge as an opportunity. Instead of asking, "Why is this happening to me?" start asking, "What can I learn from this?" or "How can this work in my favor?" That annoying colleague might teach you patience, that impossible deadline might make you more efficient, and that family gathering might just be the chance to practice your conflict resolution skills.

You can't always choose your circumstances, but you can always choose your attitude. Every difficult situation, every frustrating moment, and every irritating person in your life is a chance to grow, to learn, and to become a little more bada$$ than you were yesterday. When life hands you a mess, don't just wade through it. Dive in, splash around, and figure out how to turn that mess into something meaningful. Because at the end of the day, you have two choices: let the chaos consume you, or grab it by the horns and ride it like you were born to do it. If you're going to be here anyway, you might as well make it an adventure worth having.

Story Time

Imagine it's a crisp autumn morning, back to school season. The leaves have turned brilliant shades of orange and red, and the campus is alive with the buzz of students rushing to class. The sprawling lawns, crisscrossed by carefully planned walkways, make for a beautiful setting, but if you watch closely, something interesting is happening. A steady stream of students isn't sticking to the well-manicured sidewalks. Instead, they're cutting across the grass, forming their own route. One by one, they trek the same diagonal line between two buildings, eventually wearing down the grass, leaving a visible dirt path in their wake.

(Queue old man waving fist in the air, yelling "get off my lawn!")

This was once the situation at Michigan State University. But this phenomenon wasn't unique to MSU. Just an hour down the road, the University of Michigan was witnessing something similar. The central hub of U-of-M's campus, the Diag, a wide-open green space surrounded by buildings and the famous "M" in the middle, had its own network of walkways. The planners of the past had laid out beautifully paved paths, forming a neat crisscross pattern designed to be aesthetically pleasing and functional. But the students—well, they had other ideas. They walked where they pleased, carving out their own lines through the grass, ignoring the designers' plans entirely.

What do they say about "best laid plans"?

At both schools, these "desire paths" emerged like a silent rebellion against formality. Students, with ~~their poor time management~~ (need for efficiency) and instinctive navigation, naturally found the quickest way to get where they needed to go. It didn't take long before these unofficial routes became so well-worn that they were impossible to ignore. What had started as a few brave students cutting corners had, over time, become beaten dirt tracks that hundreds followed daily.

For a while, campus officials at both universities debated what to do. They could have easily put up signs: "Keep Off the Grass." They could have fenced off the areas to force students to stick to the paved walkways. And for a time, that's exactly what some administrators proposed. There were discussions in meetings about keeping the campus pristine, about enforcing rules to preserve the original landscape designs. After all, someone had worked hard on those campus blueprints, and students were supposed to follow them, right?

But as those desire paths continued to grow, the schools began to realize something: students weren't deliberately trying to mess up the campus. They were simply showing the most efficient way to get around. These paths weren't just shortcuts—they were the embodiment of human nature, an instinctual way to find the quickest and easiest route. So, the universities faced a choice: they could fight this natural human behavior or embrace it. In a brilliant stroke of adaptability, both MSU and U-of-M chose the latter.

At Michigan State, campus planners decided to go with the flow—literally. Instead of battling the students' foot traffic, they paved over many of these dirt trails. What had once been unsanctioned paths now became official, with fresh pavement, benches, and even lighting in some areas. The planners realized that these new routes actually made the campus more navigable. The desire paths weren't random acts of rebellion; they were practical solutions, created by the very people who needed them.

At the University of Michigan, the story was the same. The Diag, with its traditional walkways, now had new pathways that followed the students' footsteps. It wasn't about ignoring the campus's beauty; it was about understanding that function could complement form. By adopting these desire paths, U-of-M created a campus that not only looked great but worked in harmony with the habits of the people who used it. The paths were paved, benches were added, and the campus became more connected, not just in design but in spirit.

In both cases, the decision to embrace desire paths wasn't just about making life easier for students. It was a lesson in adaptability and the power of listening to human behavior. These universities realized that no matter how meticulously something is planned, people will often find their own way—and that's not a bad thing. In fact, it's how progress is made.

The lesson? Sometimes, instead of forcing people to stick to the "right" way, it's smarter to observe how they naturally navigate challenges and adapt accordingly. Whether it's a college campus or a business strategy, real innovation often comes from recognizing the paths people create for themselves and paving the way for them to thrive.

9

Words matter, still

When I say, "say what you mean without being a jerk", it means just that. So, I'm going to say it over and over again, because it's that freaking important! Saying what you mean isn't a metaphor, it's a declaration that you are going to speak with transparency and authenticity. It means not beating around the bush, being passive aggressive, vague, or manipulative. Life's too short for all that. In this book, I'm helping you to understand how to prepare someone to hear the truth, but they will never hear it if you never speak it!

Words are the common ground that binds us together. Every word we utter carries the potential to create profound impacts. They can inspire, uplift, and forge unbreakable bonds, or they can wound, isolate, and build barriers. The ridiculously uncomfortable truth is that words always matter. They are not just empty sounds or ink on a page somewhere; they are vessels of our thoughts, emotions, and intentions. The way we choose and use our words can either illuminate the path to understanding or cast shadows of confusion and misunderstanding.

It's a simple concept, but one we constantly manage to screw up. We tend to wrap our thoughts in layers of BS, sugarcoat the truth, and sprinkle in just enough vagueness to leave the other person completely lost. Like we're playing some elaborate game of charades, expecting people to guess our feelings instead of just saying them outright. Spoiler alert: No one's winning that game.

Real connection doesn't come from dancing around the point—it comes from cutting the crap and saying what you actually mean. The true art of communication is in delivering your message with razor-sharp precision, no fluff, no pretense, just raw honesty. That's how you build trust, by letting people in on what's *really* going on inside your head, not some watered-down version you think will sound better.

Think about it. How many times have you left a conversation wondering what the hell just happened, what the other person *actually* wanted, or what you were supposed to do next? That's what happens when we try to get fancy with our words and end up talking in circles. Clear communication is like handing someone a map with the destination marked out, while double-speak is like giving them a crumpled-up napkin with a vague "You figure it out" scribbled on it. Not helpful.

So, PLEASE: stop leaving people guessing. Stop with the vague hints and passive-aggressive comments that do nothing but confuse. If you want real connection, ditch the smoke and mirrors. Say what you mean. Tell them the truth, even if it's uncomfortable. That's how you get from point A to point B without getting lost in the weeds. Because, at the end of the day, precision is the fastest, most effective way to build a connection that actually means something.

Imagine words as tools within your tool belt, each one selected with care to shape an idea or emotion. When we communicate, we must be mindful of the nuances that even the simplest phrase can carry. By choosing the right words and eliminating everything unnecessary, we ensure that our message arrives with unmistakable clarity.

This doesn't mean stripping language of its richness or depth; instead, it's about using language with purpose.

So, let's make a pact, right here – right now, to say what we mean and mean what we say. Let's cut through the layers of obscurity and adornment, offering a direct path to understanding. In this way, we honor the power of words, and we honor the art of genuine connection. Clarity, after all, is the beacon that guides us through the maze of misunderstanding, leading us to a place where our words truly matter.

Zip it.

So, here's some advice that you didn't ask for but desperately need: sometimes you just need to shut up. I know, crazy concept, right? But here's the thing—knowing when to speak and when to just zip it is an underrated life skill. It's not about being passive, it's about being smart. Choose your words carefully because once you say it, there's no taking it back.

Imagine your words aren't just random noises you throw out there, but valuable currency. You wouldn't toss hundred-dollar bills out your car window (unless you're literally insane), so why are you spilling every single thought in your head like it's worth nothing? Not every situation needs commentary, and honestly, the more you talk, the less anyone actually listens. Harsh, but true. It's like the difference between throwing pebbles in a pond and tossing in a damn boulder. The fewer words, the bigger the splash.

So, here's your challenge: let silence be your secret weapon. Yeah, I know, the awkward quiet moments feel like they're going to swallow you whole, but guess what? They won't. Silence can actually speak louder than words if you use it right. Listening (truly listening) gives your words weight when you finally drop them. You don't have to comment on everything; sometimes, the most profound thing you can do is let someone else have the stage for a minute.

Not every thought you have is a precious gem, but when you curate your words like they are, people actually pay attention. Silence isn't weakness, it's strategy. Use it wisely. That way when you do speak, you're dropping boulders. Splash!

Let people shine!

Let's circle back to another topic: control. If you're out here trying to control every little thing and every person in your orbit, you're going to burn out faster than a cheap light bulb. **You're not the puppet master of the universe.** People need space to breathe, fail, learn, and yeah—sometimes totally screw up—without you hovering over them like a helicopter on a caffeine high. Newsflash: it's not your job to micromanage every detail of every moment of your life.

You think you're helping by over-communicating or double-checking everything, but really, all you're doing is smothering any chance they have to figure it out themselves. When people have room to own their roles, you're giving them the power to show up, mess up, and ultimately grow up. Trust me, no one's gonna shine if you're constantly standing in front of the spotlight.

You know what happens when you stop trying to steer every conversation and micro-correct every move? Magic. People get creative. They start taking risks (the good kind) and thinking for themselves. (Spoiler alert) That's where real growth happens. You've gotta let go of the reins and let them ride the damn horse. Sure, they might fall off a few times, but guess what? They'll learn how to ride a lot faster than if you're constantly holding the rope.

So, if you really want to be a good leader, mentor, or just a decent human being, learn to step back occasionally and let people take the wheel. Offer guidance when it's needed, but leave space for people to screw up, learn, and eventually soar on their own. Because people don't need you holding their hand every step of the way—they need you to believe they can walk.

No one is perfect.

When someone screws up, that's when your words pack the biggest punch. You can either use that moment to help them level up or knock them down a peg. But, come on, nobody's growing when they're embarrassed or feeling like crap. So, what's it gonna be? Are you going to be the person who kicks them while they're down, or are you going to be the one who helps them up?

When people mess up, they're already vulnerable. They know they blew it. Trust me, they don't need you to point it out. This is your chance to help them grow, not shrink back into avoidance of taking risk and initiative. Instead of going all-in on blame or shame, how about throwing in some understanding, maybe a little guidance, and a whole lot of "let's fix this together"? The goal isn't to make someone feel like garbage; it's to create a space where they feel like it's OK to admit they dropped the ball, learn from it, and come out swinging next time.

Look, nobody's perfect, (not either of us to be sure) and we're all going to trip up. But how we handle those mistakes, that's what separates a culture of fear from a culture of growth. Create an environment where errors are just part of the process, not something that drags people down. Because at the end of the day, mistakes are just pit stops on the road to improvement—not dead ends.

You're not that damn busy.

In the hustle of our daily lives, it's easy to get caught up in the relentless pursuit of our own priorities, to be overwhelmed by the perpetual to-do list. However, it's essential to remember that no matter how busy we may feel, there is always time to lend an ear, to be present for someone who needs to talk. Whether it's a chance encounter with a stranger at the grocery store, a friend who's going through a tough time, or a child yearning for your attention, these moments are priceless.

When we choose to offer our time and undivided attention, we are not only providing solace to those who seek it but also nurturing the bonds that tie us to the people in our lives. A kind word, a listening ear, or a comforting presence can make all the difference to someone in need. It's not just about what we say; it's about the message we send – that <u>they matter</u>, that they are valued. So, remember, when someone reaches out for a conversation, it's an invitation to be part of their world, and an opportunity to make a positive impact. It's a gift of time that costs very little to you but could mean everything to them.

Ask the damn question!

Life is full of opportunities, but often they pass us by because we hesitate to seize them. One of the most profound and yet simple truths is that if you don't ask, you don't receive. It's easy to assume that others can read our minds, that they know what we need or want, but in reality, people can't always intuit our desires. The only way to bridge this gap is to ask for what you want.

Remember - the answer to the question you never ask is always a resounding "no." By staying silent, you deny yourself the chance to make your intentions known. Whether it's a personal goal, a career opportunity, or a simple favor, you have to express your needs. This isn't about being pushy; it's about taking charge of your own life. Don't let fear of rejection hold you back. The worst that can happen is a "no," but even in that, you gain the knowledge that you tried.

There are low-calorie questions, like asking for a substitution at a restaurant, asking for something you need at a hotel, or if you can buy the floor model at a store. These are sort of no-brainers because most people out in the world are fairly accommodating and genuinely want to help. And again, the worst they could say is no, so there is huge upside potential, and almost no downside.

Then you get into the trickier questions, the ones that have some collateral attached to them. In these situations, you have to balance the weight of the answer. But there are so many times where you should just ask the damn question, even if it's hard, even if it's scary. Consider having a huge crush on someone for months. You can't stop thinking about them, you can't move on or date other people because you're holding out hope for this one person.

This is the perfect example of where you should use your words clearly to open a conversation. Potential upside, they like you too and you get exactly what you want. The downside? They could say no, but if you've crafted your message properly, without pressure or obligation, you've allowed them to decline without destroying the relationship. And, if they do say no, at least you know where you stand and you can move forward with your life. The same scenario could apply to asking for a raise or promotion. Living in limbo because you're afraid to ask a question is among the worst sort of self-inflicted punishment.

So, speak up, express your desires, and take control of your own narrative. You may be surprised at how often the world responds with a resounding "yes" when you finally ask for what you want. Communication is a tool, not a weapon. It's not about calling people out for their screw-ups or blasting them with some "tough love" excuse. It's about lifting them up, helping them see their potential when they can't, and creating an atmosphere where mistakes are just a step in the process, not the final stop.

If you've gotten this far and think, "Okay, I'll just say what's on my mind and people will get it"—nope, not quite that simple. It's about how you say it, when you say it, and why you say it. Thoughtful communication requires all of these considerations to be weighed and juggled equally.

And now that we've ripped apart the basics of not being an aSS when you talk to people, we're going to hit on a big one: **caring**. I know what you're thinking, "Everything we've been talking about is caring!" Well, not quite. You can certainly go through the motions, and cover all the bases on this, but if you don't actually genuinely care, it's going to show. I'm sure you've had conversations in the past, where people are saying all the right things, but it seemed fake as hell. You can't just fake it, people can feel it. You have to be unapologetic about giving a damn in a world where most people throw up their hands and claim they don't. So, ready or not, we're diving into what it actually means to "**care anyway**".

10

Care anyway

Everyone is on the IDGAF bandwagon these days, but you know what? I do GAF, I give a ton of F's, and you should too. Why? Because we're human, and we're all stuck here in the middle of a universe we didn't ask to be in, spinning at a thousand miles per hour, just trying to get by. Let's not make it harder than it needs to be.

What Difference Does It Make?

Oh, it makes *all* the difference. Let's cut through the nonsense – genuine connection does not happen by magic (as much as I like to pretend that it does). It happens when you give a damn about the people around you, when you decide that it's worth investing your time, energy, and emotions into understanding others. The truth is, when you care, you create a space for people to exist and be themselves. You stop forcing them into little boxes of your own expectations. Do you know what happens then?

- **More Genuine Connection:** When you care, people *feel* it. They sense that you're not just going through the motions or doing the bare minimum. They recognize that you're investing in them, and guess what? That makes them want to invest back in you. It creates a space where people can show up as they are, not as they think they *should* be. It opens the door for conversa-

tions that go beyond small talk and fake politeness. When you care, people let their guard down, and that's when the real connection happens.
- **Less Resentment:** The cold, hard truth is that resentment grows in the spaces where people feel dismissed, overlooked, or unimportant. By GAF (caring), you eliminate those spaces. You stop the passive-aggressive comments, the eye rolls, and the silent treatments before they even start. When people know you care, they're far less likely to harbor resentment because they know you see them, you hear them, and most importantly, you *value* them.

Care Anyway.

Look, it's easy to say "I don't care" or "IDGAF." It's the default setting for our generation, the go-to response when life gets tough, or people disappoint us. But, consider something else; caring takes guts. It's risky, it's messy, and sometimes, it downright sucks. But you know what sucks more? Living a life where you're constantly pretending that nothing matters. Because if you do that long enough, you start to believe it. And the moment you start believing that nothing matters is the moment you start living a life that's hollow and devoid of meaning.

So, yeah, *care anyway*. Care about the people you work with, the people you live with, and the people you randomly bump into on the street. Care about the projects you take on, the goals you set, and the promises you make. Care about the small stuff, the big stuff, and everything in between. Care, not because it's easy, but because it's worth it.

Here's a little-known secret: people can't read your mind. Shocking, I know. So, you need to COMMUNICATE. And I'm not talking about the fluffy, sugar-coated, let's-not-rock-the-boat kind of communication. I'm talking about *real*, honest, "this is what I think, feel, and need" kind of communication.

When you care enough to communicate openly, you set the stage for growth. You give others the opportunity to meet you where you are, to understand your perspective, and to share theirs in return. And that, my friend, is where the magic really happens. That's where you move from surface-level interactions to meaningful exchanges that can change the trajectory of your relationships, projects, and even your life.

Stop Pretending You Don't Care. Because You Do.

Let me hit you with some hard truth: all this "I don't care" talk is total bullshit. **Everyone cares**—they just don't want to admit it. Why? Because caring makes you vulnerable. It forces you to show up, put your ego on the line, and actually take responsibility for your relationships and your life. Guess what? That's what makes caring a damn superpower.

It's easy as hell to say, "IDGAF." It's trendy, it's cool, and it lets you dodge accountability. But deep down? You care. You care about what people think. You care about how things turn out. You care about whether or not people actually show up for you when it matters. So why pretend like you're some stone-cold robot who's above it all? Let's cut through the crap: caring is what makes life worth living.

Think about it: when you care about something—or someone—you're invested. You've got skin in the game, and that's where real progress happens. You can't build a business, a relationship, or even a decent reputation without caring. All those "too cool to care" people? They're the ones stuck in neutral, watching the rest of us who give a damn actually **make sh*t happen.**

When you care, you're committing to something. And yeah, that commitment can feel scary because it means you've got something to lose. But without that risk, there's no reward. You want strong relationships? You want success? You want people to trust you? Then start giving a damn and own it.

Caring is how you build social capital (and EVERYTHING else.)

Let's be crystal clear: caring is the cornerstone of social capital. We're not talking about fake caring, like smiling at someone just because you want something from them later. We're talking about **actually giving a sh*t** about the people in your life, the projects you take on, and the impact you make. It's the ultimate game-changer.

When you invest in people—when you show up consistently, offer support, and prove that you're someone who can be counted on—you build social capital. And that social capital? It's the difference between having a solid network that's ready to back you up and being stranded on your own when you hit a rough patch.

So if you're out there trying to convince yourself (or others) that caring is some kind of weakness, think again. Caring is your secret weapon. It's what sets you apart in a world full of people just going through the motions. People notice when you care, and they respond in kind.

Now, let's address the elephant in the room: vulnerability. I get it—you don't want to show your soft spots. But here's the thing: vulnerability isn't weakness. It's not about walking around with your heart on your sleeve, waiting to get crushed. It's about showing up as your real self, flaws and all, because that's how you form real, honest connections.

People are drawn to authenticity. They can smell a fake a mile away, and nothing makes people shut down faster than someone who's pretending not to care. On the flip side, when you're willing to **drop the act and be real**, you give other people permission to do the same. That's how trust is built. That's how collaboration happens. That's how you go from surface-level interactions to real, meaningful relationships that can weather any storm.

Let me ask you something: What kind of legacy do you want to leave? Do you want people to remember you as the person who "didn't care," who was "too cool" to engage, who sat on the sidelines while everyone else was putting in the work? Or do you want to be remembered as someone who actually gave a damn—about your team, your family, your community, and the people around you?

Because that's what caring really is: it's your impact on the world. It's how you show up. It's what you do when things get hard. It's how you treat people when they need you most. And if you're not willing to care, what are you even doing? Going through the motions? Waiting for life to just magically work itself out? Spoiler alert: **it won't.**

Caring is action. It's stepping up when it's uncomfortable, when it's risky, when it might not go the way you want. It's what separates the people who **make a difference** from the people who just sit back and watch from the sidelines. Here's the truth about caring—it's contagious. The more you care, the more people around you start to care too. They see the effort you're putting in, they feel the energy you bring, and they want to match it. That's how cultures change. That's how teams become unstoppable. That's how relationships go from being "meh" to being unbreakable.

You want a world where people care about each other, where they step up for each other and actually give a damn? Then be the one to start. Stop pretending like you're above it all. Stop acting like caring is some kind of burden. **It's not.** It's your superpower. Use it, and watch how the world around you shifts.

You want to know why most people don't care? Because they're scared. Hard stop. It's so much easier to hide behind sarcasm, indifference, or that attitude of glorified apathy. But caring requires courage – the kind of courage that's going to push you out of your comfort zone and force you to face the fact that you might not always get it right. And that's okay.

There are two types of courage in this world:

1. **Battle-Ready Courage:** This is the kind of courage where you strap on your metaphorical armor, draw your sword, and charge headfirst into the chaos. It's the courage that shows up when you have to make tough decisions, take a stand, or fight for something you believe in. It's the courage that makes you say, "I will not back down."
2. **Vulnerable Courage:** Then there's the courage that requires you to strip down, metaphorically speaking, and stand there completely exposed. This is the courage that says, "Here I am, flaws and all. Take it or leave it." It's the courage that makes you open up to others, admit when you're wrong, and show up even when you're terrified of being judged, rejected, or misunderstood.

Courage isn't about being fearless; it's about feeling the fear and still moving forward. It's about leaning into the discomfort, having tough conversations, and putting yourself out there even when there's no guarantee what's going to happen. You still may be wondering, "What's in it for me?" And here's what I'll say:

Caring isn't about *you*.

It's about creating a ripple effect that extends beyond yourself. It's about leaving the world a little bit better than you found it. Caring builds bridges instead of walls. It opens doors instead of slamming them. It creates opportunities instead of obstacles. And when you start caring, you'll find that others will start caring too. It's contagious in the best possible ways.

Action Steps – Because Caring Is a <u>Verb</u>

- **Start small:** Don't try to change the world overnight. Start by showing genuine interest in the people around you. Ask questions, listen to their stories, and make them feel heard.
- **Be present:** Put down your phone, look people in the eye, and actually *listen* when they're talking to you. It's amazing what happens when you're fully engaged.
- **Speak up:** If you see something that's not right, say something. If someone needs support, offer it. If you have something valuable to share, don't hold back. Your voice matters.
- **Own your impact:** Understand that your actions, words, and decisions have consequences. Take responsibility for the way you show up, and don't be afraid to course-correct when necessary.

So, there you have it – the unapologetic, no-nonsense truth about why you should GAF. It's not always easy, it's not always comfortable, but it's always worth it. This is how you create a life that's rich, meaningful, and full of genuine connections. And isn't that what we're all really here for?

11

It's not a fad

You've finally made it through this journey I call Kind Transparency, (I told you that you would!) and now you're equipped with the knowledge and understanding to enhance your relationships and communication. You've learned that beneath the surface of every interaction lies a world of thoughts, emotions, and desires, waiting to be uncovered and acknowledged. So, what's next on this path to fostering deeper, more authentic connections with the people around you? More work!

Put in the work every damn day.

This isn't some one and done deal. Just like you wouldn't expect to shred on the guitar after one lesson, you can't master communication without putting in the reps. Every. Single. Day. And I'm not just talking about the big, deep conversations. It's the small stuff too—your casual chats, team meetings, hell, even those awkward elevator encounters. Every interaction is a chance to practice the Kind Transparency mindset. Own it, and watch your relationships level up.

Get out there and actually *do* something.

Yeah, personal growth is great and all, but let's not pretend it's just about you. Real change? That happens when you take this mindset and plug it into the world around you. You've got the tools—now use them. Take your newfound ability to communicate openly and start applying it to your community, your workplace, your circle. Volunteer, join groups, get involved in causes that promote empathy, transparency, and real connection. Start making the world around you better. You've got a voice—use it for something bigger than yourself.

Relationships don't just happen—they're built.

Let's be honest: making real connections isn't a one-time gig. It's like lifting weights—continuous effort. Miss a few days at the gym? You're not making gains. Same with communication. You don't magically wake up one day as a master of human connection. It takes constant improvement, practice, and showing up, day after day, with intention. Every conversation you have is a chance to move the needle forward—don't waste it.

You've got time—make it count.

We all love to say, "I'm too busy," like it's a badge of honor. Cut the crap. You've got time. You're just choosing to spend it somewhere else. If you really care about building strong relationships—whether at home, at work, or with that random guy who seems pretty cool—make the damn time. Be present. Stop half-listening while checking your email. Actually focus on the person in front of you. That's how real connections are made—by showing up and giving a damn.

You're going to suck at first—keep going anyway.

Newsflash: You're going to screw up. You're going to say the wrong thing, miss a cue, or have a conversation blow up in your face. Welcome to being human. But here's the key—keep going anyway.

Just like learning a new skill, you're going to make mistakes. Those missteps? They're just lessons. The more you practice, the better you'll get. But if you throw in the towel every time something goes sideways, you're never going to build the relationships you want. Keep at it, learn, adapt, and get better every time.

Stop worrying about the "right" way—do it *your* way.

There is no one "right" way to connect with people. Stop looking for a damn script. Be yourself. Be real. That's what matters. People don't want robots, they want authenticity. So ditch the idea that you need to follow a formula to get it right. Speak your truth, communicate how you feel, and bring *your* energy into every interaction. People will respond to *you*, not the version of yourself you think they want.

People Are wildly different—adjust accordingly.

Every person is their own mixed bag of weirdness, quirks, and preferences. You can't take a cookie-cutter approach to relationships. What works with your best friend might flop with your coworker. That's okay. Pay attention to what people need, how they react, and what drives them. Adjust your communication accordingly. This isn't about being fake; it's about meeting people where they're at and building real, authentic connections.

Start small—but start NOW.

You don't have to go deep with every interaction. Start small. You're not going to turn strangers into best friends overnight. Real connections are built on small, meaningful moments. So listen. Ask questions. Give someone a genuine compliment. Offer help. These little things? They add up. They create a foundation of trust and mutual respect. From there, the deeper stuff will come naturally.

The 4 C's: Your blueprint for real connections.

Let's not over-complicate this—just follow the damn 4 C's: Communication, Collateral, Coordination, and Consistency. Speak up, and make sure your words have meaning. Balance the give and take in relationships. Make sure you're talking to the right people in the right way. And finally, keep at it. Consistency is everything. These aren't just buzzwords, they're the building blocks of every strong relationship you'll ever have.

It all starts and ends with YOU.

Before you can connect with anyone else, you've got to know your own crap first. Know your triggers, your weaknesses, your values. Understand what drives you and what pisses you off. You can't communicate well with others if you're not clear on who *you* are. So, before you look outward, take a long, hard look inward. That's where everything begins. And once you get that straight, connecting with others will feel a whole lot easier.

One last clarification: Kind Transparency isn't some fleeting trend. This isn't the latest flavor of the month that's going to disappear the moment something shinier comes along. If you've made it this far, you've probably already realized that. It's not easy, it's not always fun, and it damn sure isn't something you can fake your way through. It's about showing up—every day—and doing the real work, even when it's uncomfortable. Especially when it's uncomfortable.

This isn't a quick fix. It's not some feel-good "just be nice and everything will magically work out" BS. It's about communication that actually *means* something. It's about building connections that last because they're based on honesty, not smoke and mirrors. It's about leading with integrity and being the person people know they can rely on because you don't sugarcoat your words or hide behind pleasantries.

And guess what? It's going to challenge you. It's going to push you out of your comfort zone. You'll be forced to face the hard truths, the awkward conversations, and the moments where you'd much rather bail. But if you stick with it, if you commit to showing up authentically, you'll build relationships that matter. And isn't that what we're all after? Real connections, real trust, and real growth.

So, if you're looking for the easy way out, this isn't it. But if you're in it for the long haul, for the relationships that make life worth living, then keep going. You're on the right path. Because this? This isn't a fad. It's a way of life, and it's one that's worth every damn ounce of effort you're willing to put into it.

Closing

Here we are, it's the end of the road, but also just the beginning. Yeah, I know, it sounds like one of those motivational cat posters, but seriously look at how far you've come. You've cut through the fluff, faced some hard truths about communication, and dug deep into what it really takes to connect with people. You've embraced empathy, authenticity, and transparency like a boss, and that's no small feat.

You didn't just sit back and coast. You did the work. You leaned into the discomfort, practiced speaking up even when it was awkward, and you started to see the real impact of open, honest communication. Be proud of that. Hell, most people never even try.

But here's the thing – this isn't some one-and-done kind of deal. You don't just check the "Kind Transparency" box and move on with your life. This is the kind of work that keeps going. It's messy, it's frustrating, but with every conversation, it gets a little bit easier. Your understanding sharpens, your empathy deepens, and before you know it, this whole transparency thing? It's second nature.

You're going to mess up sometimes. You'll hit bumps in the road, run into walls, and probably want to throw your hands up and walk away more than once. But keep at it. Like anything worth doing, it takes time. You'll find that with every challenge, you're becoming more of the person who *actually* knows how to communicate—and that's powerful.

So, take a minute. Breathe. Appreciate what you've already accomplished, but don't get too comfortable. There's more work to do, more conversations to have, more connections to build. And yeah, it's going to take effort, but the ripple effect? That's where the magic happens.

Every bit of honesty you put out there spreads, touching not just your life, but the lives of everyone you interact with.

So, as you close this chapter, remember: this journey doesn't end. The world needs more people willing to be real, to be kind, and to be transparent. And you, my friend, are a vital part of that. Keep pushing, keep connecting, and don't ever forget that what you're doing matters. The world's a messy place, but with Kind Transparency, you're helping make it just a little bit better. One conversation at a time.

LFG!

Oh, and one more thing—this isn't goodbye. If you've gotten this far, you're clearly committed to making some real changes, and that's not something you have to do alone. Want to keep the momentum going? You're not off the hook yet. Connect with *Kind Transparency* online and through social media. Keep the conversation alive, share your stories, ask your questions, and get some real-time advice when you hit those inevitable roadblocks. We're building a community of people who *get it*—people who are done with the B.S. and ready to communicate, grow, and connect in real, meaningful ways.

So, don't go dark now. Hop online, follow us, and let's keep this going. After all, you didn't come this far just to come this far. Let's build something even better together. #KindTransparency

Additional Resources

Want to dive deeper and keep sharpening those *Kind Transparency* skills? We've got you covered. Scan the QR code or head over to the website to unlock bonus content and resources designed to help you take your communication game to the next level.

Whether you're looking for quick tips, real-life examples, or worksheets to keep you on track, it's all waiting for you. This isn't just a book—it's a blueprint for real change, and we're here to help you make it happen. So, don't stop now—get access to everything you need to keep pushing forward!

• • •

www.kindtransparency.com/additional-resources

Amanda Frye doesn't just "talk the talk"—she's been down in the trenches, navigating the chaotic world of tech for nearly 20 years, holding titles from Sales Coordinator to PMO Director, and pretty much everything in between. Amanda's career is a no-fluff, in-your-face journey of making things better and getting sh*t done. She's not here to sugarcoat it—whether she's leading a team or reshaping how companies approach their projects, Amanda is about driving real, measurable change.

What sets her apart? Amanda doesn't just do the work—she elevates it. She's mastered the art of cutting through the nonsense to create strategies that work and communication that's real. If you're tired of the same old small talk and want to learn how to lead with honest, no-BS transparency, Amanda's got you covered.

In *Kind Transparency*, Amanda takes everything she's learned from her roller coaster career and breaks it down into practical, actionable insights. This isn't your typical leadership book—it's the guide you didn't know you needed to cut through the noise, build better relationships, and communicate like it matters. Because it does.

Through all her roles, Amanda has always stuck to one thing—honesty. Whether she's leading teams, fixing broken processes, or mentoring the next generation of women in tech, Amanda has built her reputation on calling it like it is. *Kind Transparency* is her no-nonsense guide to mastering communication and leadership, written by someone who's lived it. If you're ready to get real about change and make a difference.

Amanda's got your back.

Notes

www.ingramcontent.com/pod-product-compliance
Lightning Source LLC
Chambersburg PA
CBHW052259220526

45471CB00001B/412